The Essential Microwave Cookbook & Guide

The Essential Microwave Recipe Book & Guide with Over 120 Quick, Easy to Follow and Mouthwatering Recipes for Beginners. Delicious and Quick Recipes for the Busy Home Cook.

Olivia Green

CONTENTS

Introduction 7

    How this book can help you to cook to perfection. 7

    So why use a microwave instead of a traditional oven? 6 reasons. 8

Using your microwave oven 10

    How do microwave ovens work? 10

    The debate about microwave cooking; is it safe? 10

What do the chefs say? 12

Conclusion 13

Breakfast Recipes 14

    Poached Eggs in The Microwave 14

    Apricot Oatmeal 15

    Egg Frittata in The Microwave 16

    French Toast 17

    Blueberry Muffin 18

    Quiche 19

    Breakfast Burrito 20

    Blueberry and Oatmeal Muffin 21

    Egg & Veggie Breakfast Bowl 22

    Cheesy Egg White and Broccoli Quiche 23

    Kale Cheese Quiche 24

    Blueberry Banana Microwave Baked Oats 25

    Homemade Omelette 26

    Quick Microwave Quiche 27

    Nutmeg Oatmeal 28

    Apple sandwich 29

    Spinach, Turkey, Mushroom and Swiss Quiche 30

    Banana-Burrito 31

    Potato-Crusted Quiche 32

    Easy Breakfast Wrap 33

Lunch Recipes 34

    Kale & Chilli Eggs 34

    Microwave Cauliflower 35

    Potato Soup 36

    Microwave Minestrone 37

    Maple Syrup-Lemon turkey Enchiladas 38

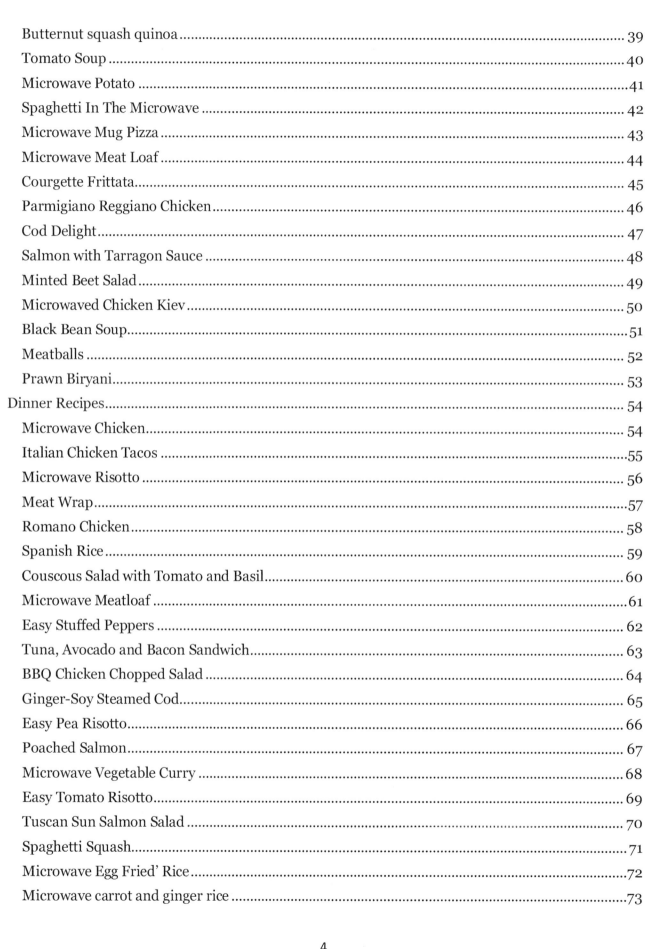

Butternut squash quinoa 39

Tomato Soup 40

Microwave Potato 41

Spaghetti In The Microwave 42

Microwave Mug Pizza 43

Microwave Meat Loaf 44

Courgette Frittata 45

Parmigiano Reggiano Chicken 46

Cod Delight 47

Salmon with Tarragon Sauce 48

Minted Beet Salad 49

Microwaved Chicken Kiev 50

Black Bean Soup 51

Meatballs 52

Prawn Biryani 53

Dinner Recipes 54

Microwave Chicken 54

Italian Chicken Tacos 55

Microwave Risotto 56

Meat Wrap 57

Romano Chicken 58

Spanish Rice 59

Couscous Salad with Tomato and Basil 60

Microwave Meatloaf 61

Easy Stuffed Peppers 62

Tuna, Avocado and Bacon Sandwich 63

BBQ Chicken Chopped Salad 64

Ginger-Soy Steamed Cod 65

Easy Pea Risotto 66

Poached Salmon 67

Microwave Vegetable Curry 68

Easy Tomato Risotto 69

Tuscan Sun Salmon Salad 70

Spaghetti Squash 71

Microwave Egg Fried' Rice 72

Microwave carrot and ginger rice 73

Snacks Recipes 74

    Microwave Caramel Popcorn 74

    Apples with Cinnamon 75

    Toast Nuts 76

    Microwave Spinach Dip 77

    Swede Chips Recipe 78

    Honey Mustard Brie with Walnuts 79

    Fruit & Granola Crisp with Yogurt 80

    Granola Cereal Bars 81

    Microwave Popcorn 82

    Microwave Polenta 83

    Baked Pears 84

    Microwave Blueberry Jam 85

    Strawberry crumble 86

    Microwave Blackberry Jam 87

    Microwave Strawberry Jam 88

    White Chocolate Truffles 89

    Béchamel Sauce 90

    Pears Crisp 91

    Microwave Sweet Potato Chips 92

    Microwave Egg Sandwich 93

Dessert Recipes 94

    Microwave Sunflower seeds Brittle 94

    Microwave Almond Butter Fudge 95

    Salted Caramel Fudge 96

    Microwave Christmas Fudge 97

    Microwave Rocky Road Fudge 98

    Fantasy Fudge 99

    Turtles 100

    Pumpkin Cake 101

    Lemon cake 102

    Churro 103

    Blondie 104

    Peanut Butter Cup 105

    Oreo Mug Cake 106

    Red Velvet Microwave Cake 107

Bread Pudding..108

Mocha Microwave Cake...109

Pumpkin Cornbread Mug Cake...110

Banana Chocolate Chip Minute Muffins...111

Chocolate Mug Cake..112

Brownie...113

Mug Meals Recipes...114

Kale ricotta Lasagne..114

Spiced Lentils...115

Easy Mac..116

Cheesy Spinach Microwave Scrambled Eggs Mug.........................117

Avocado macaroni...118

Broccoli and Cheese Rice Bowl...119

Pizza in a mug..120

Brown Rice with Edamame and Pineapple....................................121

Fettuccine Alfredo in a Mug...122

Kale Ricotta Lasagne in a Mug...123

Omelette in a Mug..124

Eggless Chocolate Mug Cake..125

Veggie Mug Omelette..126

Coffee Cup Quiche..127

Egg Mug Muffin..128

Meatloaf in a Mug...129

Cheesy homemade grits..130

Sweet potato hash...131

Chicken noodle soup...132

INTRODUCTION

This introduction explores the world of the microwave, from the earliest solo appliances, the dual-function combination machines, and right up to the top-of-the-range microwaves you can set in advance with multiple orders to defrost, cook and steam so that when you arrive home all the work is done for you.

In the days before microwave ovens, everything had to be cooked on a slow boil on hot plates or baked or roasted in a warm oven. Nowadays, alongside conventional ovens, microwaves have re-invented the world of cooking, offering home chefs an opportunity to create delicious hot food in less time. If you have just bought a microwave, congratulations, and welcome to the world of microwave cooking. With this book, you can learn how to cook a delicious meal in minutes, defrost frozen ingredients using the microwave, and then set a switch via the Wi-Fi or your phone to make soup, pasta, or any recipe, even when you are not at home.

How this book can help you to cook to perfection.

In chapter 1, we will examine the different types of the microwave oven in detail. Even for the expert in microwave cooking, this chapter shares the design features of newer models compared to older models. The first microwaves only offered a Solo option, which placed food on a revolving circular plate holder at the base of the machine. You can now choose from a wide range and sizes to suit your kitchen space. Older models were quite chunky in design and very wide on the counter whereas how the design will fit your kitchen space is a crucial part of newer models.

Convection microwave ovens use fans to circulate the microwave energy around the oven, so you have a wider choice in the menus you try. Smart microwaves allow you to operate the machine via your phone or a WiFi connection giving you even more choices of when and what to cook.

In chapter 2, you can learn various techniques on the best practice for cooking by microwave, avoiding scenarios where food hygiene is at stake. Cooking by microwave needs some instruction if you are a complete beginner. If you heat frozen food for example, often it is not cooked through evenly and may even be crispy on the outside while still frozen on the inside, which is dangerous because pathogens thrive in such environments. In chapter 2 you will certainly find up-to-date instructions for all microwaves from the simplest to the most complicated.

In the remaining chapters, there are plenty of tempting recipes to try, ranging from savoury to sweet, with step-by-step instructions and ingredient lists. In chapter 3 you can benefit from 7 useful tips to avoid the typical mistakes that cooks have with microwaves, helping you to make the best use of the new addition to your kitchen. The typical mistake that many new cooks do not know is that you cannot use metal containers in your microwave. So any user of a microwave has to learn to adapt their kitchen and perhaps buy some new cooking bowls and equipment that are suitable for this appliance.

These rules are explained in detail in chapter 4 and read on to discover why the chemistry behind metal and microwaves makes plastic bowls a better choice.

So why use a microwave instead of a traditional oven? 6 reasons.

1. *Save time.* Busy people rarely have much time to spare so if you count time as a valuable resource and any appliance that helps you to save time, then this is the main reason why microwave ovens are so popular. Microwaves are perfect for those who like to plan weekly menus in advance, using food stored in a freezer allowing anybody in the family who knows how to use the microwave to cook a pre-prepared meal for themselves. There are so many mouth-watering recipes in this book that can cook in double quantities and freeze half. You will want to get started immediately.

2. *Save money.* With gas and electricity prices rising so sharply all over the world, the second reason to use the microwave is to save energy. Cooking a roast chicken takes hours in a conventional oven and that is costing you money. Even a simple meal like a baked potato is an excellent example. The time it takes to bake a potato in a conventional oven is less than a quarter of that time in your microwave. Conventional ovens need to be heated for at least 15 minutes before cooking in order to reach the desired cooking temperature, but your microwave can set the temperature that you need, eliminating the need for waiting. Microwave cooking sets the exact temperature, defrosts the food, or cooks according to the setting and does it at record speed so your cooking does not need to break the bank.

3. *Cook straight from the freezer!* A third reason must be that you can use a microwave to defrost food easily. I remember whenever my mum was not going to be there for dinner, she used to remove cartons of frozen food from the freezer to defrost and leave complex instructions about how the whole meal should be defrosted and how germs could thrive if the meal was not completely thawed. With a microwave, no need to worry about this! This makes dinner so easy because whole meals can be frozen and then defrosted in minutes in the microwave, and then another flick of a switch, the meal is heated up and ready to serve in no time. For working parents, this means they can leave food in the freezer for their children to heat up when they get back from college or school. So nutritious home-cooked food is available at the push of a button, as long as your child can use the machine, and what child today exists that refuses to love technology? It gives teenagers a choice about what they eat too if they can choose from various meals left in a freezer. So you are teaching independence as well. You may be able to involve them in cooking and planning meals they would like to eat and give them skills for life.

4. *Retain more nutrients in food.* Fresh food has the most vitamins and nutrients. Eating fresh whenever you can ensures getting your required dose of 5-a-day essential daily vitamins and minerals. Cooking food and in particular, boiling food in a pot of water frequently boils away all this goodness. The fact that fewer nutrients and vitamins are lost in a microwave due to the speed at which it cooks food, gives the fourth reason. Think of the vegetables that have accompanied your food in cafes and restaurants or perhaps the dinners you used to get at school, where peas almost lost their green colour they were cooked for so long? You can change the timing to suit your kitchen with your microwave oven. While conventional cooking of vegetables like carrots often boils them in water for hours, the ones you cook in your microwave can be chopped evenly with a similar size to ease cooking evenly.

At the flick of a switch, they can be steamed or cooked for a shorter time making them crisp, tasty and full of the nutrients you need to stay healthy.

5. *Meals for one*. If you cook alone, you may find the whole process of cooking tiresome and even lonely. Your microwave can become a tool that enables you to cook large meals and then freeze some extra for another meal, ready to defrost in minutes. So whether you are a university student who needs a quick and easy meal or a pensioner who does not feel like cooking a meal every night, here is the answer. The recipes show the quantities clearly per person so you can double them up if you want to make extra or

6. *The melting function*. A final reason must be the super useful function that it can melt butter for cooking, melt tasks that take ages on the ring of a cooker, or be baked in the oven. Since you use only one bowl to do this, cleaning up is super easy too and if you have a dishwasher, then the dish can be popped in there, and hey presto! Hot chocolate sauce for ice cream or melted butter for pancakes or any other recipe. This is a function I use all the time and no washing up pots afterwards, which I see as a big advantage.

USING YOUR MICROWAVE OVEN

When the microwave was first invented, people were very concerned about the dangers of microwaves in our food but people now accept that using a microwave is not dangerous (unless there is an obvious break in the seal) and will certainly bring benefits to their cooking routine. The obvious use for a microwave is to defrost food but the differences in their designs now offer you a range of machines to suit you. Your microwave may be a stand-alone appliance that sits on the counter or perhaps it is under the counter, or even built-in. It has become a useful tool in any kitchen that revolutionized cooking, even for experienced chefs. See more on celebrity chefs below who love it or love to hate it!

From baking potatoes and large vegetables like butternut squash which usually takes ages, you can produce fabulous meals in a few minutes, soft and cooked to perfection. If you are vegetarian, then bean chilli can be on the menu. Learning how to cook meat, poultry, or fish is easy-peasy with our detailed recipes and guides and even a tasty risotto or pasta dish may be added to your favourite bakes. For dessert, try baking brownies, cakes, lemon rice puddings, or melted chocolate sauce for vanilla ice cream. Our recipes will inspire tasty, nutritious meals for you or a large group.

How do microwave ovens work?

The World Health Organisation (WHO) defines microwaves as high-frequency radio waves, that are part of the electromagnetic spectrum and states that all materials (including the food we want to cook in the microwave) contain water, which will easily absorb the energy and heat up, thereby cooking the food. Microwaves may be more well-known to many of you as an essential element of mobile phone technology and satellites in telecommunications. They are also utilized in medicine.

For cooking, the waves move like light does – reflecting, absorbing, or heating the materials it comes into contact with. Any food substance that contains water will react by becoming hotter, and it will cook. A word of advice about the containers used in microwave ovens though! Metal plates, saucepans, or containers cannot be used in a microwave because microwave energy is reflected by anything metallic, so the heating will not happen. However, if the food is in a plastic or glass container, it will work beautifully.

The debate about microwave cooking; is it safe?

Any reputable maker of microwave ovens must adhere to strict international standards defined by the WHO so that those microwave rays are contained within the oven. The World Health Organisation has issued a report about their safety and highlights that microwave ovens are generally safe for use, providing that they are cleaned regularly to avoid leakages from the oven into the kitchen. Checking the seals on the door initially is important and if you notice any cracks in your door, then you need to have it checked by a certified electrician before using it again. Problems with seals or open cracks could be an issue for safety if it allows the rays to escape into the kitchen and this is why your machine must be kept super clean around the door and seals.

If there is damage to either the seals or the door, then some microwave energy could escape. To prevent this, ensure that the appliance is in good working order and that it shuts correctly, and clean the door and the seals to ensure it closes tightly.

Another potential danger with microwave cooking is burning from touching either the hot, cooked food or the container it is in. Use oven gloves when handling hot food and containers and keep safe! Keep small hands away from the oven too.

Experts warn of the dangers of food that is liable to explode if it becomes overheated in a microwave too. This is due to food cooking unevenly so for example, when cooking eggs the white and yolk may cook at different rates and this can cause a mini-explosion in your oven. To avoid this, learn to follow the recommended times and try to ensure that food to be microwaved is cut into even portions so that it cooks at the same rate.

WHAT DO THE CHEFS SAY?

The Slow Cook movement may not favour the microwave and neither does Celebrity chef Gordon Ramsay, who is noted for his aversion to microwaves. He can be found on YouTube giving his opinion very loudly about some of its shortcomings. Check him out sending back food in cafes that is warm on the outside but cold on the inside or food with obvious burn marks, like on re-heated quiche, which he maintains is a sure sign that the restaurant did not prepare the food fresh but just placed a frozen portion in a microwave. I agree that the food shown did not look like a tasty dinner but provided that you learn how to use your microwave well, this should not be an issue in your kitchen.

Although it is unlikely that Mr. Ramsay would use microwaves in his Michelin-star kitchens, some chefs disagree with him. The BBC use Jack Munroe's recipes in their microwave section and for those who do not know her, Ms. Monroe has been a food writer helping people to survive on a budget for over a decade. Her hearty and filling recipes are well-loved by people in the UK. Likewise in the US, David Chang is a food broadcaster and chef whose New York restaurant, Ko, has been awarded 2 Michelin stars. Unlike Chef Ramsay, Chef Chang advocates using microwaves as an appliance that brings ease and convenience, even in a professional kitchen.

Most restaurants seem to have a badge of honour about even having a microwave in the kitchen! Many deny that they use them but there are food products that benefit from being cooked by microwave oven, not conventional ones. Take fruit, for example; its high water content means the microwaves can work perfectly, warming it up and heating it evenly to achieve a perfect texture. Other foods that benefit from microwave cooking are fish and seafood with shells, like crab and lobster, which often prove quite challenging to the inexperienced cook in an everyday kitchen. These are quite difficult to cook for even professional chefs and using conventional ovens, you may try to boil, steam or bake. The microwave approach is often to place the shelled fish in a bag or container which will steam it gently and cook it evenly. Learning the skills is possible by reading our detailed guide in chapter 2 and then following the instructions carefully in each recipe.

If you believe the microwave is only useful for defrosting food, then this book will open your eyes to a whole new world of recipes that you can use to expand your menus. From the humble baked potato topped with cheese or other delicious spicy sauces, you can experiment with grilling, roasting, making quick pasta or rice dishes, making scrumptious desserts, and even adding a cup of hot chocolate as a final touch. After cooking with our expert recipes, even the most inexperienced cook will be looking for Michelin stars from their family or household. Enjoy the cooking experience and feel free to change the tastes slightly to cater to the tastes your family enjoy most.

CONCLUSION

Whether you are an experienced microwave cooker user or a complete novice, this book is packed with tips, recipes and information to help you utilize your microwave with passion. From finding out how to actually use it, to learning how to clean it easily or which function is best used for grilling, this book provides clear instructions and recipes to use. Use the book to produce meals in minutes and this useful extra oven can help you out by saving you time and energy leaving you free to get on other tasks in your busy life.

BREAKFAST RECIPES

Poached Eggs in The Microwave

Servings 2 | Time| 05 minutes

Nutritional Content

Cal 72 | Fat 5 g | Protein 6.3 g | Carbs 0.5 g| Fiber | 0 g

Ingredients

- ❖ 2 large eggs
- ❖ 1 ml white vinegar
- ❖ 70 ml water
- ❖ salt and pepper

Directions

1. In a 170 g custard cup mix both water and white vinegar.
2. Pierce egg yolk with a toothpick, then cover loosely with plastic wrap.
3. Microwave for 1 minute or until desired doneness.
4. Adjust cooking time based on microwave power and personal preference.
5. Use a slotted spoon to quickly remove the egg from hot water to prevent further cooking.
6. Season with salt and pepper to taste before serving.

Apricot Oatmeal

Servings 1 | Time| 10 minutes

Nutritional Content

Cal 114 | Fat 1.2g | Protein 2.8 g | Carbs 25.6 g| Fiber | 4.5 g

Ingredients

- ❖ 10 g (1/4 cup) quick oats
- ❖ 75 ml water
- ❖ 35 g Apricot in juice, canned

- ❖ 1 g cinnamon
- ❖ 1 ml (1/4 tsp.) vanilla extract
- ❖ 2 g (1/2 tsp.) honey

Directions

1. Cut apricot slices into small pieces.
2. Combine oats, water, and apricot with juice in a bowl.
3. Microwave the mixture for 2 minutes, stir, and then cook for another 2 minutes using 1-minute intervals at 500 watts. For a 1200-watt microwave, heat for 30 seconds, stir, and then cook for an additional 30 seconds at 30-second intervals.
4. Sprinkle cinnamon, pour in vanilla extract, and sweeten to taste after cooking.

Egg Frittata in The Microwave

Servings 1 | Time| 06 minutes

Nutritional Content

Cal 114 | Fat 1.2g | Protein 2.8 g | Carbs 25.6 g| Fiber | 4.5 g

Ingredients

- ❖ 2 eggs
- ❖ 60 ml (4 tbsp.) coconut milk
- ❖ 40 g (1/2 cup) fresh kale leaves
- ❖ 1 tomato

- ❖ 1 -2 slices turkey bacon
- ❖ 140 g (1/3 cup) cheddar cheese
- ❖ cooking spray
- ❖ salt and pepper

Directions

1. Prepare a microwave-safe bowl by spraying it with cooking spray.
2. Wash, dry, and remove stems from kale, then tear into bite-sized pieces and add to the bowl.
3. Cut bacon into slices or cubes, and sprinkle cheese on top (use your preferred vegetables).
4. In the bowl, whisk together two eggs and milk, then gently mix with the contents at the bottom (the kale and bacon will float). Season with salt and pepper.
5. Microwave on high for 3 minutes.

French Toast

Servings 1 | Time| 07 minutes

Nutritional Content

Cal 212 | Fat 17.2g | Protein 7.8 g | Carbs 7.4 g| Fiber | 0.4 g

Ingredients

- ❖ 1 or 2 slices of bread, cubed (just fill your cup to overflowing a bit)
- ❖ 15 g (1 tbsp.) butter
- ❖ 1 egg
- ❖ 45 ml (3 tbsp.) milk
- ❖ Dash cinnamon
- ❖ Drop of vanilla extract (optional)

Directions

1. Cut bread into cubes.
2. Melt butter in a cup in the microwave for a few seconds, and spread it evenly over the cup.
3. Place some bread cubes in the cup.
4. In a separate cup, mix together the egg, milk, vanilla, cinnamon, and nutmeg. Stir well.
5. Pour the liquid mixture over the bread cubes, press down gently to let the bread absorb the liquid.
6. Microwave until the desired doneness is reached. If the center is still runny, add 10 seconds at a time after the initial minute. This should take 1 minute and 20 seconds in most microwaves.
7. Serve with syrup if desired. Enjoy!

Blueberry Muffin

Servings 1 | Time| 15 minutes

Nutritional Content

Cal 302 | Fat 15 g | Protein 4.5 g | Carbs 39.1g| Fiber | 1.4 g

Ingredients

- ❖ 30 g (1/4 cup) flour
- ❖ 1 g (1/4 tsp.) baking powder
- ❖ 15 g (1 tbsp.) brown sugar
- ❖ 30 ml (2 tbsp.) coconut milk
- ❖ 15 ml (1 tbsp.) olive oil
- ❖ 30 g (1/2 cup) blueberries
- ❖ A pinch of salt
- ❖ A pinch of vanilla extract

Directions

1. In a small bowl or cup, mix the flour, baking powder, sugar, salt, and vanilla extract.
2. Stir in the butter, milk, and olive oil (if using). Once the butter is melted, set aside.
3. For the topping, mix the flour, sugar, olive oil, and coconut flakes in another bowl.
4. Put blueberries in a mug and sprinkle with the topping.
5. Cook for 5 minutes in the microwave.
6. Before eating, carefully remove the mug and allow it cool to room temperature.

Quiche

Servings 1 | Time| 03 minutes

Nutritional Content

Cal 240 | Fat 13 g | Protein 12.6 g | Carbs 21.4 g| Fiber | 5.2 g

Ingredients

- ❖ 1 large egg
- ❖ 25 ml (1 1/2 tablespoons) whole milk
- ❖ 5 g (1 teaspoon) melted unsalted butter
- ❖ Pinch of salt
- ❖ Pinch of freshly ground black pepper

- ❖ 4 small grape tomatoes, halved
- ❖ 10 g (1/8 cup) torn pieces of fresh bread
- ❖ 15 g (1 tablespoon) grated mozzarella cheese
- ❖ 5 g (1 teaspoon) chopped fresh herbs, plus more for garnish

Directions

1. Combine egg, milk, melted butter, salt, and pepper in a microwave-safe mug. Whisk well to break up egg whites and distribute ingredients evenly.
2. Add grape tomatoes, shredded bread, grated cheese, and chopped herbs. Stir to mix.
3. Microwave for 1 minute on high until quiche is fully cooked and puffed up.
4. Serve immediately, garnished with fresh herbs.

Breakfast Burrito

Servings 1 | Time| 04 minutes

Nutritional Content

Cal 536 | Fat 20.7 g | Protein 31.1 g | Carbs 21.4 g| Fiber | 5.2 g

Ingredients

- ❖ 2 Whole eggs
- ❖ 1 Whole Wheat Tortilla
- ❖ 15 g (1/8 cup) salsa
- ❖ 50 g (1/4 cup) of Black Beans
- ❖ 30 g (1 oz.) Avocados, raw, California
- ❖ 30 ml (2 tbsp.) Milk
- ❖ 30 g (2 tbsp.) Shredded Cheddar Cheese

Directions

1. Spray a microwave-safe cup with cooking spray.
2. Mix milk and eggs and add to a cup.
3. Microwave for 45 seconds on high and stir.
4. Add black beans and stir again.
5. Microwave for an additional 30-45 seconds until almost set.
6. Put the egg and bean mixture onto a tortilla, top with salsa, shredded cheese, and diced avocado.
7. Cover and enjoy.

Blueberry and Oatmeal Muffin

Servings 1 | Time| 04 minutes

Nutritional Content

Cal 281 | Fat 8.7 g | Protein 12.2 g | Carbs 42 g| Fiber | 12.2 g

Ingredients

- 40 g (1/2 cup) dry oats
- 120 ml (1/2 cup) water
- 1 Egg
- 5 g (1 tsp) Organic Raw Honey
- 5 g (1 tsp) Baking Powder
- 5 g (1 tsp) chia seeds
- 30 g (1/5 cup) Fresh Blueberries

Directions

1. Combine oatmeal, honey, and water in a large coffee mug. Stir until oats are moist.
2. Microwave for 2 minutes on high until steaming.
3. Stir and let cool for 1 minute.
4. Add baking powder, chia seeds, and blueberries to the mixture.
5. Add 1 raw egg and mix thoroughly.
6. Microwave for 1 minute on high, watching for overflow.
7. Microwave for 20 more seconds if not firm.
8. Place mug upside down on a dish. Optional: decorate with sliced strawberries.

Egg & Veggie Breakfast Bowl

Servings 1 | Time| 10 minutes

Nutritional Content

Cal 210 | Fat 13.7 g | Protein 13.2 g | Carbs 6.1 g| Fiber | 1.7 g

Ingredients

- ❖ 5 ml (1 tsp) coconut oil
- ❖ 1 egg(s)
- ❖ 15 ml (1 tbsp.) water
- ❖ 10 g (1/4 cup) baby spinach
- ❖ 30 g (2 tbsp.) sliced mushrooms
- ❖ 30 g (2 tbsp.) part-skim shredded mozzarella cheese
- ❖ 2 cherry tomato(s)

Directions

1. Coat a custard cup with coconut oil.
2. Mix together the egg, water, spinach, and mushrooms.
3. Microwave for 30 seconds on high power. Stir and then microwave for another 30 to 45 seconds or until the egg is almost set.
4. Sprinkle cheese and tomatoes on top.
5. Serve with a slice of whole grain or gluten-free bread, if desired.

Cheesy Egg White and Broccoli Quiche

Servings 6 | Time| 60 minutes

Nutritional Content

Cal 51 | Fat 0.9 g | Protein 7.1g | Carbs 3.1 g| Fiber | 0.4 g

Ingredients

- ❖ 8 egg whites
- ❖ salt and ground black pepper, to taste
- ❖ 100 g (1 cup) broccoli florets, blanched and cooled
- ❖ 15 g (½ cup) mozzarella cheese, shredded
- ❖ 120 g (½ cup) yogurt
- ❖ 2 g (½ tsp) garlic powder
- ❖ 1 g (¼ tsp) dried thyme
- ❖ cooking spray

Directions

1. In a bowl, mix together all ingredients. Season with salt and pepper and whisk until fully combined.
2. Place the mixture in a greased microwave-safe baking dish and cook for 5 minutes or until set. This may vary depending on your microwave.
3. After baking, let the quiche cool for 10 minutes at room temperature to firm up.
4. Serve as a light breakfast or with a salad for a light lunch. Portion as desired and top with fresh parsley.

Kale Cheese Quiche

Servings 1 | Time| 05 minutes

Nutritional Content

Cal 147 | Fat 7.7 g | Protein 11.6g | Carbs 8.2g| Fiber |0.5 g

g

Ingredients

- ❖ 35 grams (1/2 cup) chopped kale
- ❖ 1 egg
- ❖ 80 grams (1/3 cup) milk

- ❖ 10 grams (1/3 cup) shredded mozzarella cheese
- ❖ salt and pepper to taste

Directions

1. Fill the mug with kale.
2. Add the milk, cheese, salt, and pepper to the mug of kale and cracked egg. Mix everything together completely.
3. Cover with a paper towel and microwave on high for 3 minutes.

Blueberry Banana Microwave Baked Oats

Servings 1 | Time| 8 minutes

Nutritional Content

Cal 369 | Fat 11 g | Protein 13.4g | Carbs 55.7 g| Fiber | 8.9 g

Ingredients

- ❖ 20 g (1/2 cup) old-fashioned rolled oats
- ❖ 15 g (1 tablespoon) ground flax seed
- ❖ 1 egg
- ❖ 120 ml (1/2 cup) coconut milk

- ❖ 40 g (1/3 banana,) mashed
- ❖ 1 g (1/4 teaspoon) cinnamon
- ❖ 10 g (2 teaspoons) honey
- ❖ 50 g (1/3 cup) fresh blueberries

Directions

1. In a medium to large microwave-safe mug or small dish, mix all ingredients except for blueberries. Then add blueberries and mix.
2. Microwave on high for 2-3 minutes. Check after 2 minutes and add an additional minute if needed.
3. Stir in additional milk, yogurt, or nut butter if desired.

Homemade Omelette

Servings 1 | Time| 08 minutes

Nutritional Content

Cal 484 | Fat 40.1 g | Protein 27.4g | Carbs 2.4 g| Fiber | 0.3 g

Ingredients

- ❖ 15 g (1 tablespoon) unsalted butter
- ❖ 6 g (1 tablespoon) chopped spring onion, optional
- ❖ 1 g (1/4 teaspoon) dried thyme
- ❖ 15 ml (1 tablespoon) whole milk
- ❖ 2 large eggs
- ❖ Pinch of kosher salt
- ❖ Pinch of freshly ground black pepper
- ❖ 55 g (1/2 cup) grated cheddar cheese

Directions

1. In a large mug, melt butter with spring onion and thyme in the microwave for 15 seconds.
2. Whisk milk and eggs until foamy.
3. Stir in cheese, pepper, and salt.
4. Microwave for another minute until the egg is cooked.
5. Serve immediately.

Quick Microwave Quiche

Servings 1 | Time| 10 minutes

Nutritional Content

Cal 378 | Fat 22.1 g | Protein 20.1g | Carbs 25 g| Fiber | 1.5 g

Ingredients

For Quiche:

- ❖ 40 g (⅓ cup) mozzarella cheese,
- ❖ 6 g (1 tbsp.) spring onion, chopped
- ❖ 2 eggs, beaten
- ❖ 80 ml (⅓ cup) milk
- ❖ 1 g (¼ tsp) salt
- ❖ 5 ml (1 tsp) hot sauce

For Crust:

- ❖ 60 g(4 tbsp.) breadcrumbs
- ❖ 10 g (2 tsp) butter

Directions

1. For the crust: In a bowl, mix butter and breadcrumbs until well combined.
2. Grease a microwave-safe baking dish with cooking spray.
3. Line the baking dish with the crust mixture.
4. Use the back of a spoon to flatten the crust in the microwave. Cook for 3 minutes on Medium, then let cool.
5. In a quiche mixture, mix eggs, milk, salt, and spicy sauce.
6. Sprinkle onion and cheese over the crust and pour the egg mixture on top.
7. Microwave for another 4 minutes on Medium until the food is fully cooked.
8. Serve with a garnish of your choice.

Nutmeg Oatmeal

Servings 1 | Time| 08 minutes

Nutritional Content

Cal 292 | Fat 2.7 g | Protein 11.5g | Carbs 55.9 g| Fiber | 5.4 g

Ingredients

- ❖ 20 g (1/2cup) quick oats
- ❖ 180 ml (3/4cup) coconut milk
- ❖ 15 ml (1tablespoon) maple syrup
- ❖ 1 pinch salt
- ❖ 4 g (1teaspoon) nutmeg

Directions

1. Combine oats and milk in the microwave and heat for 2 minutes or until desired consistency is achieved.
2. Sprinkle salt, cinnamon, and drizzle honey on top.
3. Stir and enjoy!

Apple sandwich

Servings 1 | Time| 05 minutes

Nutritional Content

Cal 356 | Fat 2.6 g | Protein 10.5 g | Carbs 78 g| Fiber | 11.5 g

Ingredients

- ❖ 1 whole wheat English muffin
- ❖ 65 g (¼ cup) plain fat-free yogurt
- ❖ 1 small apple, diced
- ❖ 30 g (2 tablespoons) dates, chopped
- ❖ 80 ml (⅓ cup) water
- ❖ 1 g (¼ teaspoon) salt

Directions

1. Place toasted English muffin halves in a bowl, face-up. Spoon cool yoghurt on top of each muffin half.
2. Chop the apple and place in a microwave-safe container with the chopped dates. Add water, season with salt and microwave for 1 minute on high. Stir, microwave for another minute, and remove from heat.
3. Pour microwaved ingredients over the yoghurt and muffins. Wait 1-2 minutes before digging in with a fork or spoon.
4. Optional: top with flavoured yoghurts, fresh fruit, or honey.

Spinach, Turkey, Mushroom and Swiss Quiche

Servings 8 | Time 3 minutes

Nutritional Content

Cal 247 | Fat 12 g | Protein 13.7g | Carbs 21.6 g| Fiber | 0.7 g

Ingredients

- ❖ 30 g (1 cup) spinach
- ❖ 210 g (1 ½ cup) turkey
- ❖ 30 g (1 cup) Italian blend cheese, shredded
- ❖ 35 g (½ cup) fresh mushrooms, sliced
- ❖ 15 g (1 tbsp.) garlic, to taste
- ❖ salt and pepper, to taste

- ❖ 5 g (1 tsp) marjoram
- ❖ 5 g (1 tsp) thyme
- ❖ 15 g (1 tbsp.) lemon pepper
- ❖ 60 g (½ cup) red onion, cooked or not
- ❖ 4 eggs, beaten well
- ❖ 185 ml (¾ cup) buttermilk
- ❖ 1 pie crust

Directions

1. To assemble the English muffin bowl, place two toasted English muffin halves in a bowl face-up. Spoon cool yoghurt on top of each muffin half.
2. To prepare the apple and date mixture, chop one apple and place it in a microwave-safe container with the dates. Add a pinch of salt and enough water to cover the ingredients. Microwave on high for one minute, stir, then microwave for another minute. Remove from heat.
3. Pour the microwaved apple and date mixture over the yoghurt and English muffins. Let sit for 1-2 minutes before digging in with a fork or spoon.
4. For extra flavour, add optional toppings such as flavored yoghurts, fresh fruit, or honey.

Banana-Burrito

Servings 1 | Time| 08 minutes

Nutritional Content

Cal 225 | Fat 9 g | Protein 5.4g | Carbs 35.1 g| Fiber | 4.3 g

Ingredients

- ❖ 1 tortilla
- ❖ 15 g (1 tablespoon) almond butter
- ❖ 10 g (2 teaspoons) jam
- ❖ 5 g (1 teaspoon) shredded coconut
- ❖ ½ medium banana

Directions

1. Spread an even layer of almond butter and jam on a tortilla, then place it on a flat surface.
2. Sprinkle coconut over the top.
3. Place a banana at one edge of the tortilla, then tightly fold it up.
4. Wrap the tortilla loosely in a paper towel and heat it in the microwave for 30-35 seconds on high.
5. Remove from the paper towel and enjoy.

Potato-Crusted Quiche

Servings 8 | Time| 35 minutes

Nutritional Content

Cal 172 | Fat 5.9 g | Protein 11.1g | Carbs 18.8 g| Fiber | 2.5 g

Ingredients

- ❖ 5 small potatoes
- ❖ 4 bacon slices cooked
- ❖ 60 g (½ cup) cheddar cheese shredded
- ❖ 240 ml (1cup) almond milk
- ❖ 5 eggs
- ❖ salt and pepper to taste
- ❖ 30 g (1/4cup) Parmigiano Reggiano cheese grated

Directions

1. Combine sliced potatoes with oil, salt, pepper, and Parmigiano Reggiano cheese in a bowl.
2. Spray a microwave-safe baking dish with cooking spray and place the mixture into the dish.
3. Flatten the mixture using the back of a spoon and microwave for 3 minutes on Medium.
4. Let it cool.
5. In a small bowl, mix the remaining ingredients.
6. Pour the liquid mixture over the partially cooked potatoes.
7. Microwave for another 4 minutes on Medium.
8. Let it cool, then slice into 8 pie slices.
9. Serve with fruit on the side.

Easy Breakfast Wrap

Servings 1 | Time| 35 minutes

Nutritional Content

Cal 251 | Fat 5.6 g | Protein 16.1g | Carbs 36.8 g| Fiber | 7.1 g

Ingredients

- ❖ 45 g (1½oz) pepper (about half a pepper), sliced
- ❖ 2 mushrooms, sliced
- ❖ 80 g (2¾oz) spinach
- ❖ pinch ground paprika
- ❖ 2 eggs
- ❖ Freshly ground black pepper
- ❖ 5 g (1 tsp) freshly chopped parsley
- ❖ 1 tortilla wrap

Directions

1. In a microwave-safe dish, combine the peppers, mushrooms, and paprika. Microwave on high for 2-3 minutes, or until the vegetables are soft.
2. Crack the eggs into the dish with the vegetables and stir to scramble. Microwave on high for 1-2 minutes, stirring every 30 seconds, until the eggs are cooked.
3. Warm the tortilla in the microwave for 10 seconds on high.
4. To assemble the wrap, place the egg and vegetable mixture on the tortilla, fold up one end, and then tuck in the sides. Serve immediately.

LUNCH RECIPES

Kale & Chilli Eggs

Servings 1 | Time| 05 minutes

Nutritional Content

Cal 205 | Fat 9.9 g | Protein 14.2 g | Carbs 16.8 g| Fiber | 1.9 g

Ingredients

- ❖ Handful of kale, finely chopped
- ❖ ½ small red chilli, deseeded and chopped
- ❖ 200 g can of chopped tomatoes
- ❖ squeeze of lemon juice
- ❖ 2 medium eggs, yolks and whites separated

Directions

1. In a microwave-safe bowl, mix kale, tomatoes, chillies, lemon juice, and salt.
2. Push the mixture to the sides, create a well in the center. Cover with cling film and microwave on medium heat for 40 seconds.
3. Let it cool briefly before adding egg whites.
4. Pierce egg yolks to prevent them from exploding when combined with the egg whites.
5. Microwave for another 40 seconds.
6. Remove cling film, sprinkle with black pepper, and serve.

Microwave Cauliflower

Servings 2 | Time| 15 minutes

Nutritional Content

Cal 134 | Fat 7.5 g | Protein 5.8 g | Carbs 15.6 g| Fiber | 7.3 g

Ingredients

- ❖ 1 medium head cauliflower
- ❖ 15 ml (1 tablespoon) olive oil
- ❖ 15 ml (1 tablespoon) freshly squeezed lemon juice
- ❖ 2 g (½ teaspoon) kosher salt
- ❖ 1 g (¼ teaspoon) freshly ground black pepper

Directions

1. Start by trimming and cleaning the cauliflower. Cut it into florets.
2. Take a sizable microwave-safe bowl and add the cauliflower florets. Pour in 60 ml (1/4 cup) of cold water.
3. Cover the bowl with plastic wrap or a microwave-safe plate (make sure it doesn't touch the cauliflower).
4. Microwave the bowl on high for around 10 minutes, until the cauliflower is tender-crisp. Use oven mitts to remove the bowl from the microwave and place it on a trivet. Carefully remove the plate and cling wrap, as hot steam will escape from the bowl.
5. Season the cauliflower with salt, pepper, lemon juice, and extra virgin olive oil according to your preference. Serve immediately.

Potato Soup

Servings 1 | Time| 08 minutes

Nutritional Content

Cal 236 | Fat 14.5 g | Protein 13.8 g | Carbs 13 g| Fiber | 1.3 g

Ingredients

- ❖ 170 g (¾ cup) water
- ❖ 45 g (3 tablespoons potatoes) in small cubes
- ❖ 15 g (1 tablespoon) white onion, chopped
- ❖ 30 g (2 tablespoons) cheddar cheese
- ❖ 1 bacon, cooked

- ❖ 10 g (2 tsp) cornflour
- ❖ 115 ml (½ cup) chicken stock (or vegetable stock)
- ❖ 55 ml (¼ cup) milk
- ❖ Salt & pepper
- ❖ Sour cream for garnish, optional

Directions

1. In a microwave-safe cup, combine water and potatoes. Microwave for 3-4 minutes, stirring halfway through.
2. Drain the cooking water.
3. Mix in bacon, cheese, onions, and cornflour to thicken the soup.
4. Pour in milk and stock. Season with salt and pepper.
5. Microwave for 2 1/2 to 3 minutes until the soup thickens and heats through. Keep a close eye on the mug to avoid overcooking or spills.
6. Garnish with sour cream, bacon, and chives before serving.

Microwave Minestrone

Servings 5 | Time| 30 minutes

Nutritional Content

Cal 272 | Fat 4.6 g | Protein 14.9 g | Carbs 43.8 g| Fiber | 11.3 g

Ingredients

- 250 g (1 cup) each sliced parsnips, leek, and Courgette
- 100 g (1/2 cup) diced any colour pepper
- 1 onion
- 15 ml (1 tablespoon) coconut oil
- 425 g (1 can (15 ounces) butter beans, rinsed and drained
- 400 g (1 can (14-1/2 ounces)) chicken broth
- 400 g (1 can (14-1/2 ounces)) diced tomatoes, undrained
- 130 g (1 cup) macaroni, cooked and drained
- 4 g (1 teaspoon) dried oregano
- 2 g (1/2 teaspoon) salt
- 1 g (1/4 teaspoon) pepper

Directions

1. Combine parsnips, leek, courgette, pepper, and onion in a microwave-safe 2-qt. bowl. Pour oil on top and swirl to coat.
2. Microwave covered on high for 3 minutes. Stir with remaining ingredients and microwave covered on high for 9-11 minutes.

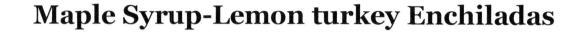

Maple Syrup-Lemon turkey Enchiladas

Servings 6 | Time| 30 minutes

Nutritional Content

Cal 300 | Fat 10.2 g | Protein 18.4 g | Carbs 35.2 g| Fiber |3.6 g

Ingredients

- ❖ 85 g (1/4 cup) maple syrup
- ❖ 30 ml (2 tablespoons) orange juice
- ❖ 15 ml (1 tablespoon) olive oil
- ❖ 10 g (2 teaspoons) paprika
- ❖ 1 g (1/4 tsp.) minced garlic
- ❖ 450 g (3 cups) turkey breast, cooked
- ❖ 500 g (2 cans) red enchilada sauce
- ❖ 12 tortillas
- ❖ 85 g (3/4 cup) Mozzarella cheese

Directions

1. In a large bowl, mix together maple syrup, orange juice, olive oil, chili powder, and minced garlic. Add turkey and coat it with the mixture.
2. Oil a microwave-safe plate and place one can of red enchilada sauce on it. Spread 1/4 cup of the turkey mixture on each tortilla in a random pattern.
3. Roll up the tortillas and place them seam side down in the prepared dish. Use any extra enchilada sauce to top them off. Cover and microwave on high for 11-13 minutes or until fully cooked. Add grated cheese on top and sprinkle with tomatoes and green onions if desired.

Butternut squash quinoa

Servings 4 | Time| 20 minutes

Nutritional Content

Cal 272 | Fat 3. 5 g | Protein 7.1 g | Carbs 55.8 g| Fiber | 1.5 g

Ingredients

- ❖ 250 g quinoa
- ❖ 700 ml hot chicken stock
- ❖ 1 medium butternut squash

- ❖ big handful grated Parmigiano Reggiano
- ❖ handful coriander leaves, roughly chopped

Directions

1. Combine quinoa and 500 ml of hot stock in a large bowl.
2. Microwave wrapped in plastic on high for five minutes.
3. Peel and cut squash into medium-sized pieces.
4. Mix rice before adding squash and remaining stock.
5. Microwave covered for an additional 15 minutes, stirring once, until tender and almost all stock absorbed.
6. Let sit for 2 minutes, then add Parmigiano Reggiano and coriander. Add more shredded cheese on top before serving.

Tomato Soup

Servings 2 | Time| 05 minutes

Nutritional Content

Cal 215 | Fat 12.3 g | Protein 8.3 g | Carbs 18.5 g| Fiber | 3.3 g

Ingredients

- ❖ 250 ml (1 cup) marinara sauce
- ❖ 120 ml (1/2 cup) chicken broth
- ❖ 60 ml (1/4 cup) heavy cream or whole milk
- ❖ 30 g (2 tablespoons) grated Parmigiano Reggiano cheese
- ❖ 1 g (1/4 teaspoon) salt
- ❖ 1 pinch black pepper

Directions

1. Mix the ingredients and cover with a moist paper towel before microwaving for two to three minutes.
2. To enhance the flavor, top the dish with croutons or serve with grilled cheese.

Microwave Potato

Servings 1 | Time| 15 minutes

Nutritional Content

Cal 478 | Fat 21.5 g | Protein 13 g | Carbs 60.5 g| Fiber | 6.7 g

Ingredients

- ❖ 1 large russet potato
- ❖ 15 g (1 tablespoon) butter
- ❖ 50 g (3 tablespoons) shredded Cheddar cheese
- ❖ salt and pepper to taste
- ❖ 15 g (1 tablespoon) sour cream
- ❖ Chopped spring onions

Directions

1. Begin by washing and scrubbing the potato thoroughly, then pierce it multiple times with a fork. Place it on a serving dish.
2. Microwave the potato at maximum power for five minutes. After five minutes, flip the potato and microwave for an additional five minutes.
3. Once the potato is soft, remove it from the microwave and cut it in half lengthwise.
4. Add salt and pepper to taste, then use a fork to crush the inside of the potato. Sprinkle cheese and butter on top and microwave for 1 minute to melt the cheese.
5. Finally, garnish with sour cream and spring onions, then serve.

Spaghetti In The Microwave

Servings 1 | Time| 10 minutes

Nutritional Content

Cal 288 | Fat 2.3 g | Protein 11.3 g | Carbs 54.7 g| Fiber | 0 g

Ingredients

- ❖ 100 g spaghetti (dry)
- ❖ 400 ml water

Directions

1. Place dried spaghetti in a microwave-safe bowl.
2. Ensure spaghetti is fully covered with water before adding more.
3. Microwave spaghetti on high for the recommended time on package plus three more minutes.
4. Stir spaghetti halfway through cooking to prevent sticking if making multiple dishes.
5. Check doneness of spaghetti and cook longer if needed.
6. Drain water using a sieve.
7. Mix spaghetti with your preferred sauce, which can be reheated in the microwave.

Microwave Mug Pizza

Servings 1 | Time| 05 minutes

Nutritional Content

Cal 491| Fat 33.5 g | Protein 17 g | Carbs 29.5 g| Fiber | 1.3 g

Ingredients

- ❖ 60 g (4 tablespoons) plain flour
- ❖ ¼ g (1/16 teaspoon) baking soda
- ❖ ½ g (1/8 teaspoon) salt
- ❖ 45 ml (3 tablespoons) coconut milk
- ❖ 15 ml (1 tablespoon) pizza sauce
- ❖ 15 g (1 tablespoon) shredded cheddar cheese
- ❖ 15 ml (1 tablespoon) oil
- ❖ 5 mini sausages
- ❖ ½ g (1/8 teaspoon) baking powder
- ❖ 2 g (1/2 teaspoon) dried Italian seasoning

Directions

1. In a microwave-safe cup, mix together baking powder, salt, baking soda, and flour.
2. Add milk and oil, then combine. It's okay if there are lumps.
3. Use a spoon to spread pizza sauce over the top of the batter.
4. Add cheese, sausage, and dry spices as a garnish.
5. Microwave the cup for 1 minute 10 to 1 minute 20 seconds. Stop when the toppings start to bubble and the batter rises. (Note: The timing may vary depending on your microwave's wattage.)
6. Enjoy your dish immediately!

Microwave Meat Loaf

Servings 4 | Time| 15 minutes

Nutritional Content

Cal 428 | Fat 9.5 g | Protein 39.9 g | Carbs 44.5 g| Fiber | 2.3 g

Ingredients

- ❖ 1 egg
- ❖ 75 g (5 tablespoons) Barbecue Sauce, divided
- ❖ 30 g (2 tablespoons) Dijon mustard
- ❖ 54 g (1/2 cup) crackers crumbs
- ❖ 30 g (2 tablespoons) onion soup mix
- ❖ 1 g (1/4 teaspoon) salt
- ❖ 1 g (1/4 teaspoon) pepper
- ❖ 450 g (1 pound) ground turkey
- ❖ 60 g (1/4 cup) sugar
- ❖ 30 g (2 tablespoons) brown sugar
- ❖ 30 ml (2 tablespoons) Balsamic vinegar

Directions

1. Combine egg, barbecue sauce, cracker crumbs, dry soup mix, salt, and pepper in a large bowl. Add turkey crumbles and mix. Form mixture into an oval loaf.
2. Place loaves in a microwave-safe dish and cover. Microwave on high for 10-12 minutes or until no longer pink and thermometer reads 70° C (160° F).
3. Drain.
4. Sprinkle ketchup, vinegar, and sugars on top of meatloaf. Microwave covered on high for an additional 2-3 minutes. Let rest for 10 minutes before cutting.

Courgette Frittata

Servings 4 | Time| 25 minutes

Nutritional Content

Cal 211 | Fat 14.6 g | Protein 14.9 g | Carbs 6.2 g| Fiber | 1.6 g

Ingredients

- ❖ 500 g (4 cups) finely chopped Courgette (3-4 medium)
- ❖ 1 small onion, chopped
- ❖ 4 large eggs
- ❖ 3 g (3/4) teaspoon salt
- ❖ ½ g (1/8 teaspoon) pepper
- ❖ 115 g (1 cup) shredded cheddar cheese

Directions

1. In a microwavable pan, combine courgette and onion. Cover and microwave on high for 3-4 minutes until tender.
2. Drain.
3. In a separate bowl, whisk together eggs, salt, and pepper. Add cheese and stir.
4. Slowly pour mixture over the zucchini mixture in the pie pan.
5. Microwave at 70% power for 8-9 minutes, or until a knife inserted in the centre comes out clean.

Parmigiano Reggiano Chicken

Servings 2 | Time| 10 minutes

Nutritional Content

Cal 301 | Fat 15 g | Protein 42 g | Carbs 1.5 g| Fiber | 0.1 g

Ingredients

- ❖ 2 (115 g) boneless skinless chicken breast halves (4 ounces each)
- ❖ 15 ml (4 teaspoons) reduced-sodium soy sauce
- ❖ 1 g (1/4 teaspoon) garlic powder
- ❖ ½ g (1/8 teaspoon) pepper
- ❖ 10 g (1/4 cup) grated Parmesan cheese
- ❖ 5 g (1 teaspoon) butter

Directions

1. Put the chicken in a dish that can be microwaved.
2. Add soy sauce, pepper, and garlic powder on top.
3. Add cheese and butter, then sprinkle.
4. For 4-5 minutes on high, with the lid on, or until the internal temperature reaches 70°C.

Cod Delight

Servings 4 | Time| 15 minutes

Nutritional Content

Cal 162 | Fat 8.1 g | Protein 20.4 g | Carbs 2.5 g| Fiber | 0.5 g

Ingredients

- ❖ 1 small tomato, chopped
- ❖ 55 g (1/3 cup) finely chopped onion
- ❖ 30 ml (2 tablespoons) water
- ❖ 30 ml (2 tablespoons) canola oil
- ❖ 20 ml (4 to 5 teaspoons) lemon juice
- ❖ 4 g (1 teaspoon) dried parsley flakes
- ❖ 2 g (1/2 teaspoon) dried basil
- ❖ 1 small garlic clove, minced
- ❖ ½ g (1/8 teaspoon) salt
- ❖ 4 cod fillets (115 g each)
- ❖ 4 g (1 teaspoon) seafood seasoning

Directions

1. Combine the first nine ingredients in a small bowl. Put the cod in a baking dish and spread tomato sauce on top. Sprinkle with seafood seasoning.
2. Cover the dish and cook the salmon in the microwave on high for 5-6 minutes, or until it flakes easily with a fork.

Salmon with Tarragon Sauce

Servings 4 | Time| 20 minutes

Nutritional Content

Cal 72 | Fat 5 g | Protein 6.3 g | Carbs 0.5 g| Fiber | 0 g

Ingredients

- ❖ 4 salmon fillets (170 g each)
- ❖ 1 g (1/4 teaspoon) salt
- ❖ 1 g (1/4 teaspoon) white pepper
- ❖ 30 ml (2 tablespoons) chicken broth
- ❖ 15 g (1 tablespoon) butter

- ❖ 1 spring onion, finely chopped
- ❖ 15 g (1 tablespoon) plain flour
- ❖ 5 g (1 teaspoon) Dijon mustard
- ❖ 2 g (1/2 teaspoon) dried tarragon
- ❖ 160 ml (2/3 cup)2% milk

Directions

1. Grease a microwave-safe dish and place the salmon inside. Sprinkle salt and pepper on top, then pour wine over the fish.
2. Cover the dish and microwave for 4-6 minutes, or until the salmon flakes easily with a fork.
3. Once done, keep it warm.
4. In the same pan juices, add butter and onion.
5. Cover the dish and microwave for 1 minute.
6. In a separate bowl, mix the flour, mustard, and tarragon.
7. Gradually add milk to the mixture and stir every 30 seconds.
8. Cook without a cover for 1-2 minutes, or until the sauce thickens. Serve the sauce together with the salmon.

Minted Beet Salad

Servings 6 | Time| 25 minutes

Nutritional Content

Cal 85 | Fat 5.4 g | Protein 1.5 g | Carbs 8.9 g| Fiber | 2 g

Ingredients

- ❖ 5 beet roots
- ❖ 30 ml (2 tablespoons) water
- ❖ 30 ml (2 tablespoons) rice vinegar
- ❖ 30 ml (2 tablespoons) avocado oil
- ❖ 2 g (1/2 teaspoon) salt
- ❖ 1 g (1/4 teaspoon) ground pepper
- ❖ 45 g (1/4 cup) Capers, quartered
- ❖ 5 g (2 tablespoons) fresh mint, divided

Directions

1. Remove one-inch-tall tops from cleaned beets. Place them in a big microwave-safe dish with a little water. Cook covered on high for 14-15 minutes, turning once, and let stand for 5 minutes.
2. Peel and cut the beets into chunks after they cool.
3. Mix oil, salt, pepper, and vinegar in a bowl.
4. Add beets, capers, and 1 tablespoon of mint.
5. Cover the bowl and let it cool in the refrigerator for at least an hour.
6. Sprinkle the remaining tablespoon of mint on top before serving.

Microwaved Chicken Kiev

Servings 4 | Time| 30 minutes

Nutritional Content

Cal 333 | Fat 20.5 g | Protein 33.7 g | Carbs 2.5 g| Fiber | 1.8 g

Ingredients

- ❖ 75 g (5 tablespoons) butter, softened, divided
- ❖ 2 g (1/2 teaspoon) minced chives
- ❖ 1 g (1/4 teaspoon) garlic powder
- ❖ 1 g (1/4 teaspoon) white pepper

- ❖ 4 boneless skinless chicken breast halves (120 g each)
- ❖ 30 g (1/3 cup) cornflake crumbs
- ❖ 15 g (1 tablespoon) grated Parmigiano Reggiano cheese
- ❖ 2 g (1/2 teaspoon) dried parsley flakes
- ❖ 1 g (1/4 teaspoon) paprika

Directions

1. In a small bowl, combine 3 tablespoons of butter, chives, garlic powder, and pepper. Form the mixture into four cubes and freeze for about 10 minutes until firm.
2. While waiting, flatten the chicken breast halves.
3. Place one cube of butter in the center of each breast and fold the long sides over the butter. Secure the ends with a toothpick.
4. Combine cornflakes, cheese, parsley, and paprika in a small bowl. Melt any remaining butter. Dip the chicken in the butter and coat it uniformly with the cornflake mixture. Place the chicken in a microwave-safe dish, seam side down.
5. Cook the chicken, uncovered, on high for 5-6 minutes, or until the thermometer registers 170° and the chicken juices flow clear. Remove the toothpicks and drizzle the pan drippings over the chicken if desired.

Black Bean Soup

Servings 2 | Time| 10 minutes

Nutritional Content

Cal 411 | Fat 11.2 g | Protein 26 g | Carbs 54.5 g| Fiber |12.5 g

Ingredients

- ❖ 130 g (3/4 cup) canned black beans, rinsed, and drained
- ❖ 180 ml (3/4 cup) chicken broth
- ❖ 45 g (1/3 cup) salsa
- ❖ 60 g (1/4 cup) whole kernel corn

- ❖ Dash hot pepper sauce
- ❖ 5 g (1 teaspoon) lime juice
- ❖ 55 g (1/2 cup) shredded cheddar cheese
- ❖ 15 g (1 tablespoon) chopped spring onion

Directions

1. Mix the first five ingredients in a bowl that can be used in a microwave.
2. When heated all the way through, cover and microwave on high for 2 minutes.
3. Pour into two serving bowls and add lime juice to each.
4. Add cheese and spring onions as garnish.

Meatballs

Servings 8 | Time| 20 minutes

Nutritional Content

Cal 533 | Fat 35 g | Protein 45 g | Carbs 25 g| Fiber | 4.5 g

Ingredients

- ❖ 900 g (2 pounds) frozen cooked meatballs, thawed
- ❖ 2 medium parsnips
- ❖ 1 small onion,
- ❖ 1 small pepper, julienned
- ❖ 1 garlic clove,

- ❖ 285 ml (1 jar (10 ounces)) sweet-and-sour sauce
- ❖ 20 g (4-1/2 teaspoons) coconut aminos
- ❖ Hot cooked quinoa

Directions

1. Put the meatballs, parsnips, onion, pepper, and garlic in a 3-qt. container safe for the microwave.
2. Mix coconut aminos and sweet-and-sour sauce in a small bowl and pour over meatballs.
3. Cover the meatballs and microwave them on high for 6 to 8 minutes, tossing twice until everything is heated thoroughly and the vegetables are mushy.
4. Serve the dish with quinoa.

Prawn Biryani

Servings 2 | Time| 2 hr.05 minutes

Nutritional Content

Cal 902 | Fat 30.5 g | Protein 19.3 g | Carbs 135 g| Fiber | 7.3g

Ingredients

- 250 g (1 ⅓ cups) uncooked white rice
- 255 g (9 ounces) prawns
- 15 g (1 tablespoon0 ginger garlic paste
- 5 g (1 teaspoon) garam masala
- 5 g (1 teaspoon) ground black pepper
- 4 whole cloves
- 4 whole cardamom seeds
- 2 cinnamon sticks
- salt to taste
- 120 g (½ cup) plain yogurt
- 55 ml (¼ cup) vegetable oil
- 240 ml (1 cup) water
- 2 cubes chicken bouillon

Directions

1. Combine rice with enough water to cover in a small bowl. Soak for two hours, then drain.
2. In a microwave-safe bowl, mix prawns, ginger garlic paste, garam masala, black pepper, cloves, cardamom seeds, cinnamon sticks, salt, yoghurt, and oil. Stir well. Microwave on High for 10 minutes until the prawns turn pink and are no longer translucent. Remove the prawns from the curry and set them aside.
3. Mix the curry with rice, water, and chicken bouillon. Microwave on High for 10 minutes. Add the prawns and microwave on High for 5 minutes, or until heated. Remove the cinnamon stick, cloves, and cardamom seeds before serving.

DINNER RECIPES

Microwave Chicken

Servings 5 | Time| 15 minutes

Nutritional Content

Cal 512 | Fat 18.4 g | Protein 69.3 g | Carbs 15.9 g| Fiber | 2.3g

Ingredients

- ❖ 240 g (1 cup) ketchup
- ❖ 30 g (5 tablespoons) curry powder
- ❖ 5 g (1 teaspoon) cayenne pepper
- ❖ 8 chicken legs

Directions

1. In a microwave-safe casserole dish, mix together ketchup, curry powder, and cayenne powder. Add chicken chunks and toss to coat.
2. Arrange the thin section of chicken legs in a fan-like pattern at the center of the dish.
3. Cover the dish and microwave on high for 12 to 15 minutes or until the chicken is cooked through and the juices run clear.

Italian Chicken Tacos

Servings 4 | Time| 25 minutes

Nutritional Content

Cal 504 | Fat 27 g | Protein 29.3 g | Carbs 38.9 g| Fiber | 8g

Ingredients

- ❖ 30 g (½ cup) Italian dressing mix
- ❖ 60 g (¼ cup) Greek yogurt
- ❖ 30 g (1 (1 ounce)) packet taco seasoning mix,
- ❖ 15 g (1 tablespoon) cheese dip
- ❖ 290 g (2 cups) shredded grilled chicken
- ❖ 8 almond flour tortillas
- ❖ shredded romaine
- ❖ 1 tomato
- ❖ 4 spring onions, sliced
- ❖ 115 g (1 (4 ounce) can) sliced Capers
- ❖ 113 g (1 cup) shredded mozzarella cheese

Directions

1. Start by combining 1 tsp of taco spice, Greek yoghurt, Italian dressing, and cheese dip in a mixing bowl. Once combined, chill it and cover with a lid until ready to eat.
2. Take the remaining taco spice and mix it with the chicken. Then, use parchment or kitchen roll to loosely wrap the bowl. Place the bowl in the microwave and heat for two to three minutes until the chicken is thoroughly cooked.
3. To soften the tortillas, heat them in a skillet for about a minute on each side. Once heated, add a spoonful of chicken, romaine, tomatoes, spring onions, capers, and cheese on top of the tortilla. Finish by drizzling Italian dressing over the top.

Microwave Risotto

Servings 4 | Time| 15 minutes

Nutritional Content

Cal 316 | Fat 9.8 g | Protein 6 g | Carbs 42.2 g| Fiber | 1.9g

Ingredients

- ❖ 45 g (3 tablespoons) butter
- ❖ 1 clove garlic, minced
- ❖ 1 onion, chopped
- ❖ 360 ml (1 ½ cups) vegetable broth
- ❖ 185 g (1 cup) uncooked Arborio rice
- ❖ 80 ml (¾ cup) white wine
- ❖ 10 g (¼ cup) grated Parmesan cheese

Directions

1. In a 3-quart microwave-safe casserole dish, combine butter, garlic, and onion. Microwave on high for three minutes.
2. Place vegetable broth in a microwave-safe dish and heat until hot but not boiling (about 2 minutes).
3. Add rice and stock to the casserole dish with the onion, butter, and garlic. Cover tightly and microwave on high for 6 minutes.
4. Combine rice and wine and cook on high for an additional ten minutes. Allow most of the liquid to evaporate.
5. Serve rice after mixing in the cheese.

Meat Wrap

Servings 1 | Time| 10 minutes

Nutritional Content

Cal 883 | Fat 33.5 g | Protein 29.3 g | Carbs 122.5 g| Fiber | 17.3g

Ingredients

- ❖ 1 (10-inch) corn tortilla
- ❖ 4 slices roast chicken
- ❖ 15 g (½ cup) shredded mozzarella- cheese
- ❖ 30 g (½ cup) shredded lettuce
- ❖ 90 g (½ cup) tomato
- ❖ 30 g (¼ cup) onion
- ❖ 4 capers
- ❖ 30 g (2 tablespoons) salad dressing

Directions

1. Place the tortilla on a dish and then add the roast chicken on top of the cheese-covered tortilla. If necessary, microwave the cheese for 45 seconds to melt it.
2. Use lettuce, tomato, onion, and capers as a garnish and sprinkle 3 or 4 dashes of dressing on top.
3. Complete the dish.

Romano Chicken

Servings 6 | Time| 25 minutes

Nutritional Content

Cal 269 | Fat 13.5 g | Protein 28.9 g | Carbs 6.9 g| Fiber | 0.7g

Ingredients

- ❖ 4 skinless, boneless chicken breast halves - pounded to 1/4-inch thickness
- ❖ 115 g (¼ pound) Swiss cheese, sliced
- ❖ 115 g (¼ pound) ham, sliced thin
- ❖ 30 g (2 tablespoons) grated Parmigiano Reggiano
- ❖ 10 g (1 ½ teaspoons) paprika
- ❖ 2 g (½ teaspoon) garlic salt
- ❖ 2 g (½ teaspoon) dried tarragon
- ❖ 2 g (½ teaspoon) dried basil leaves
- ❖ 15 g (1 tablespoon) butter, melted
- ❖ 35 g (⅓ cup) dry breadcrumbs

Directions

1. Place the chicken breasts on a pan. Roll up the Swiss cheese and ham pieces, securing them with toothpicks if needed.
2. In a small bowl, mix breadcrumbs, Parmesan cheese, paprika, garlic salt, tarragon, and basil. Dip the rollups into the mixture to coat.
3. Drizzle melted butter over the rollups and cook on High in the microwave for 4 minutes or until the chicken is cooked through.

Spanish Rice

Servings 4 | Time| 40 minutes

Nutritional Content

Cal 372 | Fat 12.5 g | Protein 15.5 g | Carbs 48.3 g| Fiber | 2.2g

Ingredients

- ❖ 6 slices bacon, chopped
- ❖ 185 g (1 cup) white rice
- ❖ ½ onion, chopped
- ❖ 500 g (1 (19 ounce) can) whole peeled tomatoes
- ❖ 240 ml (1 cup) water
- ❖ ¼ cup diced green pepper
- ❖ 60 g (¼ cup) ketchup
- ❖ 5 g (1 teaspoon) salt
- ❖ 2 g (½ teaspoon) chili powder
- ❖ 1 dash ground black pepper

Directions

1. Place bacon in a microwave-safe 2-quart baking dish and microwave for approximately 6 minutes until crispy. Transfer bacon to a platter.
2. Combine rice and onion in the same baking dish and microwave for 4 minutes or until soft. Add cooked bacon, tomatoes, ketchup, water, green pepper, salt, and pepper. Cover and microwave for 10 minutes. Stir occasionally and continue to cook for 8 minutes or until rice is cooked and flavors are well-balanced.
3. Let the dish cool briefly before serving.

Couscous Salad with Tomato and Basil

Servings 6 | Time| 25 minutes

Nutritional Content

Cal 214 | Fat 4.1 g | Protein 7.3 g | Carbs 36.6 g| Fiber | 2.9g

Ingredients

- ❖ 15 ml (1 tablespoon) extra-virgin olive oil
- ❖ 2 cloves garlic, minced
- ❖ 410 g (1 (14.5 ounce) can) fat-free, reduced-sodium chicken broth
- ❖ 260 g (1 ½ cups) couscous
- ❖ 360 g (2 cups) chopped tomato
- ❖ 2 g (⅓ cup) thinly sliced fresh basil

- ❖ 30 ml (2 tablespoons) balsamic vinegar
- ❖ 2 g (½ teaspoon) salt
- ❖ 1 g (¼ teaspoon) ground black pepper
- ❖ 15 ml (1 tablespoon) extra-virgin olive oil
- ❖ 40 g (¼ cup) crumbled feta cheese

Directions

1. Put 1 tablespoon of olive oil and garlic in a big microwave-safe bowl. Microwave on high for 45 seconds until it smells good. Add chicken broth and microwave on high for 4 minutes until simmering. Stir and add couscous. Cover and wait for 5 minutes until the liquid is gone. Fluff up the couscous with a fork.
2. Combine tomato, basil, vinegar, salt, and black pepper to prepare couscous.
3. Add the other tablespoon of olive oil, then feta cheese.

Microwave Meatloaf

Servings 8 | Time| 40 minutes

Nutritional Content

Cal 267 | Fat 9.3 g | Protein 32.3 g | Carbs 12.1 g| Fiber | 1.3g

Ingredients

- ❖ 225 g (1 (8 ounce) can) tomato sauce
- ❖ 55 g (¼ cup) brown sugar
- ❖ 4 g (1 teaspoon) prepared mustard
- ❖ 1 medium onion, minced
- ❖ 60 g (½ cup) cracker crumbs
- ❖ 40 g (¼ cup) minced green pepper

- ❖ 2 large eggs, lightly beaten
- ❖ 5 g (1 teaspoon) salt
- ❖ 2 g (¼ teaspoon) ground black pepper
- ❖ 2 g (¼ teaspoon) garlic powder
- ❖ 900 g (2 pounds) extra lean ground beef

Directions

1. Combine brown sugar, mustard, and tomato sauce until sugar dissolves.
2. In a large mixing bowl, stir together onion, cracker crumbs, bell pepper, eggs, salt, pepper, and garlic powder. Add ground beef and half of the tomato sauce mixture. Transfer to a 2-quart microwave-safe baking dish and spread remaining tomato sauce mixture on top.
3. Microwave on high for 10-15 minutes until set, clear fluids, and no pink meat. Use an instant-read thermometer to ensure the internal temperature is 75°C (165°F).
4. Drain any remaining grease and let sit uncovered for 10-15 minutes before serving.

Easy Stuffed Peppers

Servings 4 | Time| 30 minutes

Nutritional Content

Cal 153 | Fat 3g | Protein 7.2g | Carbs 26.4 g| Fiber | 4g

Ingredients

- ❖ 2 large red peppers, halved and seeded
- ❖ 230 g (1 (8 ounce) can) stewed tomatoes, with liquid
- ❖ 60 g (⅓ cup) quick-cooking brown rice
- ❖ 30 ml (2 tablespoons) hot water
- ❖ 2 spring onions, thinly sliced
- ❖ 40 g (½ cup) frozen corn kernels, thawed and drained
- ❖ 200 g (½ (15 ounce)) can kidney beans, drained and rinsed
- ❖ 1 g (¼ teaspoon) crushed red pepper flakes
- ❖ 15 g (½ cup) shredded mozzarella cheese
- ❖ 15 g (1 tablespoon) grated Parmigiano Reggiano

Directions

1. Place pepper halves in a glass baking dish.
2. Cover the dish with plastic wrap and poke a few vent holes in it.
3. Microwave for 4 minutes or until peppers are soft.
4. In a medium bowl, combine rice, water, and tomato juice. Microwave for 4 minutes or until fully cooked. Cover with plastic wrap.
5. Mix tomato mixture with spring onions, corn, kidney beans, and red pepper flakes. Microwave for 3 minutes or until heated through.
6. Top pepper halves evenly with the hot tomato mixture and wrap with plastic wrap. Poke a few holes in the plastic to release steam.
7. Microwave for 4 minutes.
8. Remove plastic wrap, sprinkle with mozzarella and Parmigiano Reggiano cheese, and let stand for 1 to 2 minutes before serving.

Tuna, Avocado and Bacon Sandwich

Servings 2 | Time| 10 minutes

Nutritional Content

Cal 798 | Fat 46.4g | Protein 49.3 g | Carbs48.5 g| Fiber | 8.5g

Ingredients

- ❖ 4 slices bacon
- ❖ 140 g (1 (5 ounce)) can solid white tuna packed in water
- ❖ 2 g (½ teaspoon) Dijon mustard
- ❖ 2 g (½ teaspoon) prepared horseradish
- ❖ 15 g (1 tablespoon) sweet pickle relish
- ❖ 15 g (1 tablespoon) minced red onion
- ❖ 1 g (¼ teaspoon) paprika
- ❖ black pepper to taste
- ❖ 2 hoagie buns, split
- ❖ 1 avocado - peeled, pitted and sliced
- ❖ 1 tomato, sliced
- ❖ 2 slices cheddar cheese
- ❖ 2 lettuce leaves

Directions

1. Place bacon on a platter coated with paper towels and cook in the microwave for about 4 minutes until crispy.
2. Combine tuna, Dijon mustard, horseradish, relish, and red onion. Add pepper and paprika for flavour. Divide mixture among hoagie buns.
3. On each sandwich, add 2 slices of bacon, 1 lettuce leaf, 1 slice of provolone cheese, 1/2 an avocado, 1/2 a tomato, and 1 lettuce slice.

BBQ Chicken Chopped Salad

Servings 6 | Time| 20 minutes

Nutritional Content

Cal 732 | Fat 13.2 g | Protein 37 g | Carbs 135.7 g| Fiber | 26.1g

Ingredients

- ❖ 1 head romaine lettuce, chopped
- ❖ 425 g (1 (15 ounce)) can black beans, rinsed and drained
- ❖ 425 g (1 (15 ounce)) can sweet corn, drained
- ❖ 1 red bell pepper, chopped
- ❖ 110 g (1 cup) peeled, shredded Mexican turnip
- ❖ 120 g (1 cup) shredded carrots
- ❖ 4 scallions, thinly sliced
- ❖ Handful of (¼ cup) chopped fresh basil
- ❖ Handful of (¼ cup) chopped fresh cilantro
- ❖ 3 limes, divided
- ❖ 170 g (1 (6 ounce)) package cooked chicken breast strips
- ❖ 2 tablespoons barbeque sauce
- ❖ 1 avocado - peeled, pitted, and cubed

Directions

1. Combine lettuce, black beans, corn, red bell pepper, jicama, carrots, onions, basil, and cilantro in a sizable bowl. Drizzle the juice of two limes over the salad and toss gently.
2. Combine chicken and barbecue sauce in a microwave-safe bowl. Heat in the microwave for about 45 seconds until chicken is heated through.
3. Place the remaining lime over the salad and add chicken, avocado, and remaining ingredients on top.

Ginger-Soy Steamed Cod

Servings 4 | Time| 35 minutes

Nutritional Content

Cal 218 | Fat 5.7 g | Protein 22.7 g | Carbs 18.4 g| Fiber | 1.2g

Ingredients

- ❖ 70 g (1 bunch) cabbage
- ❖ 1 clove garlic
- ❖ 4 spring onions
- ❖ 5 ml (1 tsp.) sesame oil
- ❖ 30 ml (2 tbsp.) coconut aminos
- ❖ 15 ml (1 tbsp.) apple cider vinegar
- ❖ 10 g (2 tsp.) fresh ginger paste
- ❖ 4-piece skinless, boneless cod fillet
- ❖ 2 package rice

Directions

1. Cut cabbage into 1-inch pieces and rinse well in cold water to remove any sand.
2. Place cabbage in a colander to drain and rinse with fresh water as needed. Do not spin dry.
3. Microwave cabbage and half of the garlic in a microwave-safe bowl on High for 4-5 minutes, covered with vented plastic wrap. Let it sit covered.
4. Slice the white and light-green parts of remaining spring onions into 1-inch pieces, saving the dark-green tips for later.
5. In a 9-inch glass pie plate, microwave remaining garlic and spring onion pieces with sesame oil for 2-3 minutes on High, covered with vented plastic wrap.
6. Place cod fillet on top of the onion mixture, folding thin ends under for even thickness. Stir coconut aminos, vinegar, and ginger into the onion mixture. Microwave cod on High for 4-5 minutes, covered with vented plastic wrap, until just becoming opaque throughout. Let sit covered for 2 minutes.
7. Cook rice as directed on the package in the microwave.
8. To serve, divide cabbage onto four plates. Top with fish, pie plate liquid, and saved spring onion tips. Serve with rice on the side.

Easy Pea Risotto

Servings 4 | Time| 30 minutes

Nutritional Content

Cal 476 | Fat 2.5 g | Protein 16.8 g | Carbs 94.8 g| Fiber | 9g

Ingredients

- ❖ 590 g (1 can) chicken broth
- ❖ 570 ml (2 1/4 cups plus 2 tablespoons) water
- ❖ 450 g (1 lb.) frozen peas
- ❖ 15 ml (1 tbsp.) olive oil
- ❖ 370 g (2 cup) Arborio rice
- ❖ 15 g (1/2 cup) freshly grated Parmigiano Reggiano

Directions

1. In a 2-quart covered pan, bring chicken broth and water to a boil.
2. While the broth is boiling, put peas and 2 tablespoons of water in a large microwave-safe bowl. Cover with vented plastic wrap and microwave on High for 4 minutes. Blend peas with 1/4 cup of the hot broth mixture in a blender until smooth. Keep the leftover peas aside.
3. Combine rice and olive oil in a 3 1/2 to 4-quart microwave-safe basin. Cook uncovered on High for 1 minute. Add the remaining hot broth mixture and stir. Cover with vented plastic wrap and microwave on Medium (50 percent power) for 10 minutes, stirring once.
4. Add the pea puree and simmer for an additional 8 minutes on Medium (50 percent power) until most of the liquid is absorbed. Add the Parmesan, remaining peas, and 1/4 teaspoon each of salt and freshly ground pepper.
5. Spoon risotto into 4 small dishes for serving and top with Parmigiano Reggiano.

Poached Salmon

Servings 4 | Time| 15 minutes

Nutritional Content

Cal 276 | Fat 12 g | Protein 41.2 g | Carbs 1.4 g| Fiber | 0.4g

Ingredients

- ❖ 1 lemon
- ❖ 4 skinless centre-cut salmon fillets
- ❖ 1 g (1/4 tsp.) salt
- ❖ 60 ml (1/4 cup) water
- ❖ 4 whole cloves

Directions

1. Place lemon slices in a single layer in a 20 cm x 20 cm glass baking dish. Add salmon fillets on top and sprinkle with salt. Add water to the dish.
2. Cover the dish with vented plastic wrap and cook on High for 8 minutes. When the fish starts to become slightly opaque, remove it from the dish using a slotted spatula and drain on paper towels.
3. Let the salmon cool for 15 minutes or until it reaches room temperature.

Microwave Vegetable Curry

Servings 2 | Time| 60 minutes

Nutritional Content

Cal 500 | Fat 37.9 g | Protein 8.1 g | Carbs 40.3 g| Fiber | 12.8g

Ingredients

- ❖ 100 g (3½ oz) frozen spinach
- ❖ 15 ml (1 tbsp.) sunflower oil
- ❖ 10 g (3 tbsp.) medium Indian curry paste,
- ❖ 1 onion, finely chopped
- ❖ 375 g (13 oz) butternut squash,
- ❖ 400 g (7 oz) tin coconut milk,
- ❖ 100 g (3½ oz) frozen peas

Directions

1. Place frozen spinach in a microwave-safe bowl and heat on high for 2 minutes. Set aside.
2. In a sizable microwave-safe mixing bowl, combine oil, curry paste, onion, and squash. Cover the bowl with a plate and microwave on high for 10 minutes or until the squash is soft.
3. If using coconut milk, scoop out the solid, thick coconut cream from the top of the tin and add it to the curry. Add the frozen peas and spinach (along with any liquid).
4. After an additional 5 minutes of cooking under the plate cover in the microwave, thoroughly heat the meal. Serve with microwaved rice or heated naan bread.

Easy Tomato Risotto

Servings 6 | Time| 40 minutes

Nutritional Content

Cal 377 | Fat 7.1 g | Protein 10.8 g | Carbs 69.3 g| Fiber | 7.1g

Ingredients

- ❖ 1 bag microwave-in-bag green beans
- ❖ 420 ml (1 3/4 cup) vegetable broth
- ❖ 480 ml (2 cups) water
- ❖ 30 g (2 tbsp.) butter
- ❖ 1 small onion
- ❖ 370 g (2 cups) arborio rice
- ❖ 900 g (2 lb.) ripe tomatoes
- ❖ 240 g (2 cups) fresh corn kernels
- ❖ 60 g (2 oz.) finely grated Parmesan cheese
- ❖ 10 g (2 tbsp.) chopped basil
- ❖ salt
- ❖ pepper

Directions

1. Boil broth and water in a 2-litre saucepan.
2. Soften butter and onion in a 4-litre microwave-safe bowl on high for 3 minutes. Mix in rice for 1 minute on high heat.
3. Mix rice and broth together. Cover with vented plastic wrap and microwave for 10 minutes on medium (50% power).
4. Puree half the tomatoes in a food processor. Strain liquid through a sieve into a measuring cup, discarding solids. Chop remaining tomatoes.
5. Mix rice and tomato juice. Cover with vented plastic wrap and microwave for 5 minutes on medium until most liquid is absorbed.
6. Mix in corn, cover with vented plastic wrap, and microwave for 3 minutes on medium or until corn is heated.
7. Add Parmesan, tomatoes, green beans, half of the basil, 1/2 tsp salt, and 1/4 tsp pepper to the risotto. Garnish with fresh basil.

Tuscan Sun Salmon Salad

Servings 4 | Time| 15 minutes

Nutritional Content

Cal 262 | Fat 16.5 g | Protein 23.7 g | Carbs 5.7 g| Fiber | 1.9g

Ingredients

- ❖ 1 lemon
- ❖ 60 ml (1/4 cup) water
- ❖ 4 skinless salmon fillets
- ❖ 1 g (1/4 tsp.) salt
- ❖ Freshly ground black pepper
- ❖ 140 g (5 oz.) baby arugula
- ❖ 75 g (1/2 cup.) red peppers

- ❖ 70 g (1/2 cup) Kalamata olives
- ❖ 15 ml (1 tbsp.) balsamic vinegar
- ❖ 10 ml (2 tsp.) extra-virgin olive oil

Directions

1. Place lemon slices in a single layer in a glass baking dish measuring 20 by 20 cm.
2. In step 2, add 60ml of water. Before serving, add 1/4 teaspoon of salt and 1/8 teaspoon of freshly ground black pepper to the thawed salmon.
3. Microwave the fish on high for 8 minutes, covered with vented plastic wrap, until it just begins to become opaque throughout. Meanwhile, in a large bowl, mix baby arugula, Kalamata olives, roasted red peppers, balsamic vinegar, and extra virgin olive oil.
4. Divide the mixture evenly among 4 dishes and top with salmon.

Spaghetti Squash

Servings 4 | Time| 35 minutes

Nutritional Content

Cal 108 | Fat 4.9 g | Protein 1.6 g | Carbs 17.3 g| Fiber | 0g

Ingredients

- ❖ 2 spaghetti squash (about 2 pounds or 1 kilo each)
- ❖ 15 ml – 30 ml (1-2 tablespoons) olive oil
- ❖ Salt and ground black pepper, to taste

Directions

1. Begin by washing the outside of the squash. Cut the squash lengthwise from stem to tail. If the stem is too hard to cut around, trim the ends. Remove and discard the seeds in the centre of each half with a spoon.
2. Place the squash cut-side down in a microwave-safe baking dish that can fit 2 halves.
3. Add about 1 inch of water to the dish to create steam in the microwave.
4. After 15 minutes on HIGH in the microwave, check to make sure the squash is soft enough.
5. If the squash is not fully cooked, microwave for an additional five minutes to make the centre soft.
6. Carefully remove the squash from the microwave and allow it to cool before handling.
7. To create spaghetti strands, use a fork to scrape the food.

Microwave Egg Fried' Rice

Servings 1 | Time| 40 minutes

Nutritional Content

Cal 902 | Fat 30.5 g | Protein 19.3 g | Carbs 135 g| Fiber | 7.3g

Ingredients

- ❖ 125 g (4½ oz) cold cooked rice
- ❖ 1 spring onion, finely chopped
- ❖ 80 g (3 oz) frozen peas
- ❖ 5 g (1 tsp) reduced salt soy sauce
- ❖ 1 egg
- ❖ 6 g (1 tbsp.) roughly chopped fresh coriander
- ❖ salt and freshly ground black pepper

Directions

1. In a microwave-safe bowl, mix together the rice, peas, spring onions, and soy sauce.
2. Crack the egg into the bowl and stir, breaking apart the yolk and incorporating it into the rice.
3. Cover the bowl with a piece of kitchen paper and microwave on high for 2 minutes, or until the egg is cooked and the dish is heated through.
4. Mix in half of the coriander and season with salt and pepper, then sprinkle the remaining coriander on top before serving.

Microwave carrot and ginger rice

Servings 2 | Time| 60 minutes

Nutritional Content

Cal 212 | Fat 2.5 g | Protein 4.9 g | Carbs 45.7 g| Fiber | 3.6g

Ingredients

- ❖ 2 scallions
- ❖ 1 garlic clove,
- ❖ 5 g (1 tsp) ginger,
- ❖ 2 carrots,
- ❖ 250 g (9 oz) cooked basmati rice,
- ❖ 5 ml (2 tsp) coconut aminos

- ❖ 5 ml (2 tsp) maple syrup
- ❖ 5 ml (2 tsp) vinegar
- ❖ 5 g (1 tbsp.) roughly chopped fresh coriander
- ❖ 5 g (1 tsp) sesame seeds
- ❖ 1 lemon, halved

Directions

1. Combine all ingredients except for the limes, sesame seeds, and half of the coriander in a large microwave-safe bowl.
2. Microwave on high for 3 minutes or until heated through, covering the dish with paper towels.
3. Stir in the lime juice, divide the mixture into serving bowls, and garnish with the remaining coriander and sesame seeds.

SNACKS RECIPES

Microwave Caramel Popcorn

Servings 16 | Time| 15 minutes

Nutritional Content

Cal 123 | Fat 6 g | Protein 0.9 g | Carbs 17.5 g| Fiber | 0.9 g

Ingredients

- ❖ 200 g (8 cups) cooked popcorn
- ❖ 220 g (1 cup) coconut sugar
- ❖ 115 g (1/2 cup) butter
- ❖ 80 ml (1/4 cup) maple syrup
- ❖ 2 g (1/2 teaspoon) salt
- ❖ 5 g (1 teaspoon) vanilla extract
- ❖ 2 g (1/2 teaspoon) baking soda

Directions

1. Put the popped popcorn into a large bag.
2. Combine the butter, maple syrup, salt, vanilla, and coconut sugar in a 1.9-liter dish or heat-resistant serving bowl.
3. Microwave the mixture for three minutes, stirring in between each minute. Mix well before adding baking soda.
4. Close the top of the bag after coating the popcorn with the syrup. Shake the bag thoroughly to distribute the syrup evenly.
5. Microwave the bag for one minute and ten seconds on high power. Shake the bag well before microwaving it for another minute and ten seconds.
6. Spread the popcorn on a piece of parchment or wax paper.
7. Let the coated popcorn cool and solidify. Enjoy!

Apples with Cinnamon

Servings 1 | Time| 05 minutes

Nutritional Content

Cal 120 | Fat 0.5 g | Protein 0.6 g | Carbs 31.5 g| Fiber | 5.7 g

Ingredients

- ❖ 1 small apple -
- ❖ 15 g (1 tablespoon) coconut sugar
- ❖ 1 g (¼ teaspoon) cinnamon
- ❖ 1 g (¼ teaspoon) corn starch
- ❖ 15 ml (1 tablespoon) water

Directions

1. Core, peel, slice, or dice the apples and place them in a freezer-safe plastic bag with the other ingredients.

2. Close the bag and shake vigorously to mix the ingredients. Alternatively, combine all ingredients in a microwave-safe bowl and cover loosely.

3. To vent, slightly reopen the bag. Microwave on High for 2 minutes, or longer if using a large apple.

4. Pour the hot contents of the bag over plain or cinnamon-sugar pita chips, flour tortilla chips or oatmeal with caution.

Toast Nuts

Servings 8 | Time| 60 minutes

Nutritional Content

Cal 184 | Fat 16.8 g | Protein 4.4 g | Carbs 6.8 g| Fiber | 1.9g

Ingredients

- ❖ 215 g (1.5 cup) mixed nuts like - almonds, walnuts, seeds
- ❖ 20 g (1/2 cup) oatmeal

Directions

1. Take a microwave-safe plate and evenly distribute the following ingredients: pecans, almonds, walnuts, seeds (e.g. sunflower or pumpkin seeds), oats, and coconut.
2. Microwave on HIGH for one minute, then stir the mixture.
3. If the nuts, seeds, oats, or coconut aren't toasted properly yet, repeat step #2 until they are. This should take around 2-3 minutes in total.

Microwave Spinach Dip

Servings 10 | Time| 10 minutes

Nutritional Content

Cal 103 | Fat 9.1 g | Protein 4.3 g | Carbs 2.1 g| Fiber | 0.8g

Ingredients

- ❖ 300 g (12 oz.) spinach
- ❖ 15 ml (1 tablespoon) lemon juice
- ❖ 225 g (8 oz) cream cheese
- ❖ 120 ml (1/2 cup) milk
- ❖ 50 g (2 cups). grated mozzarella
- ❖ garlic salt to taste

Directions

1. Microwave the spinach, covered, for 2 minutes in a microwave-safe container. To prevent bursting, make sure to open the box or pierce the bag several times.
2. Allow the spinach to cool for a few seconds.
3. Squeeze handfuls of spinach over a sink or bowl until most of the liquid is drained.
4. Place the drained spinach in a bowl.
5. Heat lemon juice, water chestnuts, milk, and cream cheese in a medium bowl, covered, for 1 minute on high. Whisk after removing from microwave.
6. Add spinach, mozzarella, garlic salt, and a few drops of Tabasco to the cream cheese mixture.
7. Fold all the ingredients together.
8. Microwave the covered bowl for 1 minute.
9. Stir, then cook in the microwave for 1 minute and 30 seconds. All ingredients should be hot and melted together.
10. If desired, transfer to a serving bowl and serve immediately.

Swede Chips Recipe

Servings 2 | Time| 60 minutes

Nutritional Content

Cal 358 | Fat 3.9 g | Protein g | Carbs 74.4 g| Fiber | 9.4g

Ingredients

- ❖ 4 medium swede
- ❖ 5 g (1 1/2 teaspoon) salt
- ❖ 120 ml (1/2 cup) virgin olive oil

Directions

1. Wash and peel the potatoes under running water. Slice thinly and place in a glass basin. Brush olive oil on the sliced potatoes and add salt. Toss thoroughly.
2. Cook the coated potatoes on high for 3-4 minutes until dry and crisp on a microwave-safe plate. Remove and let them cool. Store in an airtight container.
3. Serve as a teatime snack with tea or coffee.

Honey Mustard Brie with Walnuts

Servings 6 | Time| 15 minutes

Nutritional Content

Cal 212 | Fat 2.5 g | Protein 4.9 g | Carbs 45.7 g| Fiber | 3.6g

Ingredients

- ❖ 200 g (7 oz) Brie or Camembert
- ❖ 20 ml (1½ tbsp) honey Dijon mustard
- ❖ 50 ml (¼ cup) finely chopped walnuts or pecans
- ❖ 1 apple and pear slices
- ❖ Crackers

Directions

1. Spread mustard on the sides of the cheese using a spatula. Roll the sides in chopped nuts to coat them. Sprinkle the remaining nuts on top and spread the remaining mustard.

2. Put the nut-coated cheese on a microwave-safe serving plate. Microwave on Medium-Low (30%) for 1 1/2 to 2 1/2 minutes, or until the cheese is warm and softened.

3. Arrange crackers, apple and pear pieces around the cheese. Serve immediately.

Fruit & Granola Crisp with Yogurt

Servings 4 | Time| 10 minutes

Nutritional Content

Cal 223 | Fat 2.7 g | Protein 4.3 g | Carbs 47.6 g| Fiber | 3g

Ingredients

- ❖ 500 g (3 cups) sliced apricots,
- ❖ 145 g (1 cup) raspberries,
- ❖ 165 g (4 tablespoons) butterscotch ice cream topping
- ❖ 50 g (4 tablespoons) granola
- ❖ 450 g (2 cups) Greek yogurt

Directions

1. Divide the apricots and raspberries evenly into four 225-gram ramekins.
2. Sprinkle granola and butterscotch on top of each ramekin. Microwave, uncovered, for one to two minutes on high power, or until it starts to bubble.
3. Finish by adding a tablespoon of Greek yoghurt to each ramekin.

Granola Cereal Bars

Servings 12 | Time| 15 minutes

Nutritional Content

Cal 184 | Fat 7.7 g | Protein 4.5 g | Carbs 26 g| Fiber | 2g

Ingredients

- ❖ 110 g (1/2 cup) packed brown sugar
- ❖ 130 g (1/2 cup) creamy peanut butter
- ❖ 80 g (1/4 cup) light corn syrup
- ❖ 5 g (1 teaspoon) vanilla extract

- ❖ 80 g (2 cups) old-fashioned oats
- ❖ 60 g (1-1/2 cups) crisp rice cereal
- ❖ 20 g (1/4 cup) miniature chocolate chips

Directions

1. Combine 100g of brown sugar, 200g of peanut butter, and 120ml of corn syrup in a microwave-safe bowl.
2. Cover the bowl and microwave on high for 2 minutes, or until the mixture boils, stirring once.
3. After mixing of oats and of cereal, add 5ml of vanilla.
4. Add of chocolate chips and fold into the mixture. Grease a 20cm square pan with cooking spray and press the mixture into it.
5. Allow to cool, then slice into bars.

Microwave Popcorn

Servings 5 | Time| 10 minutes

Nutritional Content

Cal 48 | Fat 1.1 g | Protein 1.9 g | Carbs 9.2 g| Fiber | 1.6g

Ingredients

- ❖ 50 g (¼ cup) popcorn kernels
- ❖ ½ tsp. canola oil

Directions

1. Mix popcorn kernels and oil in a medium glass bowl that can be used in a microwave.
2. Cover with a plate and heat on High for 3 to 4 minutes, or until pops last about 3 seconds.
3. Take the plate out slowly.
4. Salt to taste and serve.

Microwave Polenta

Servings 4 | Time| 15 minutes

Nutritional Content

Cal 108 | Fat 1.5 g | Protein 3.9 g | Carbs 20.3 g| Fiber | 1.6g

Ingredients

- ❖ 480 ml (2 1/4 up). boiling water
- ❖ 240 ml (1 cup) coconut milk
- ❖ 90 g (3/4 cup) yellow cornmeal
- ❖ 8 g (1 1/2 tsp.) salt

Directions

1. In a large microwave-safe bowl or casserole, stir boiling water, milk, cornmeal, and salt. Cover with waxed paper and cook on High for 5 minutes.
2. Remove from the microwave and whisk the mixture vigorously until it is smooth. It may be lumpy at first.
3. Cover the mixture and return to the microwave on High for an additional 2 to 3 minutes until it thickens.
4. Whisk the mixture once and you will have 3 cups.

Baked Pears

Servings 2 | Time| 10 minutes

Nutritional Content

Cal 114 | Fat 3.5 g | Protein 4 g | Carbs 1.7 g| Fiber | 3.6g

Ingredients

- ❖ 2 pears
- ❖ 30 g (2 tbsp.) sugar
- ❖ 5 g (1 tsp.) ground cinnamon
- ❖ 5 g (1 tsp.) ground nutmeg
- ❖ 10 g (2 tsp.) butter

Directions

1. Do not remove the bottom of the pears.
2. Mix together sugar, cinnamon, and nutmeg in a bowl. Sprinkle half of the sugar mixture over the pears and add one teaspoon of butter on each pear. Place the pears in a microwave-safe casserole dish and cover.
3. Microwave for 3 1/2 to 4 minutes, or until the pears are soft.
4. Let the pears sit for two minutes before serving.

Microwave Blueberry Jam

Servings 8 | Time| 60 minutes

Nutritional Content

Cal 110 | Fat 0.2 g | Protein 0.4 g | Carbs 28.7 g| Fiber | 0.6g

Ingredients

- ❖ 250 g (2 cup) fresh blueberries
- ❖ 220 g (1 cup) sugar
- ❖ 15 ml (1 tbsp.) lemon juice

Directions

1. Combine blueberries, sugar, and lemon juice in a microwave-safe bowl. Microwave on high for 10 minutes, stirring every 1-2 minutes (more often towards the end of cooking) until thickened. Test readiness by placing 1 tsp of jam on a cooled saucer.
2. Briefly freeze the jam until slightly chilled. Gently push with your finger.
3. If the surface wrinkles, it's ready.
4. Transfer the jam to a sterilized jar.

Strawberry crumble

Servings 2 | Time| 10 minutes

Nutritional Content

Cal 150 | Fat 2.5 g | Protein 4.9 g | Carbs 15.7 g| Fiber | 2.6g

Ingredients

- ❖ 250 g (1 cup) strawberries,
- ❖ 2 g (1/2 tsp) vanilla extract
- ❖ 4 ml (1 tsp) lemon juice
- ❖ 50 g (1/4 cup) honey
- ❖ 100 g (1/3 cup Honey Granola Clusters

- ❖ 4 chocolate wafers
- ❖ 150 g (2/3 cup) thick pudding mix, to serve
- ❖ 2 g (1/2 tsp) honey, to serve

Directions

1. In a 1-liter microwave-safe dish, blend strawberries, vanilla essence, lemon juice, and honey.
2. Combine 100g of chocolate wafers and granola in a separate bowl. Sprinkle the mixture over the strawberries.
3. Microwave the dish on HIGH for 2 minutes.
4. Transfer the mixture to serving dishes and top with a dollop of pudding mix and additional honey.

Microwave Blackberry Jam

Servings 2 | Time| 20 minutes

Nutritional Content

Cal 212 | Fat 2.5 g | Protein 4.9 g | Carbs 45.7 g| Fiber | 3.6g

Ingredients

- ❖ 500g (5 cups) blackberries
- ❖ 300 g (1 1/2 cups) caster sugar
- ❖ 25 ml (1/3 cup) lemon juice

Directions

1. Put blackberries, sugar, and lemon juice in a large, heatproof, microwave-safe bowl.
2. Microwave the mixture, uncovered, for 4 minutes on 100% power. Stir once every minute until the sugar dissolves.
3. Microwave the mixture on high (100%) for 17 to 18 minutes. Stir every four minutes until the jam reaches setting point. Wait for two minutes until the bubbles stop. Spoon the jam carefully into a heated and sterile jar.
4. Seal and let it cool.
5. Store the jam in the refrigerator for up to one month after opening.

Microwave Strawberry Jam

Servings 8 | Time| 45 minutes

Nutritional Content

Cal 163 | Fat 0.2 g | Protein 0.5g | Carbs 43 g| Fiber | 1.6g

Ingredients

- ❖ 500 g (5 cups) strawberries, washed, hulled, chopped
- ❖ 300 g (1 ½) cups white sugar
- ❖ 1 large lemon, juiced

Directions

1. Put strawberries in a 3-liter heatproof bowl that may be used in a microwave (such as Pyrex). Sprinkle in sugar and 1/3 cup of lemon juice. Uncovered, use HIGH (100%) power for 4 minutes in the microwave. Stir.
2. Continue to microwave at HIGH (100%) power for a further 15 minutes, or until the jam reaches the setting point (see hint). Fill hot, sterile jars with hot jam. Seal. Jars should be upside-down for two minutes. Right side up, then.
3. Cool.
4. Store the jam in the refrigerator for up to one month after opening.

White Chocolate Truffles

Servings 36 | Time| 60 minutes

Nutritional Content

Cal 55 | Fat 3 g | Protein 0.9 g | Carbs 45.7 g| Fiber | 3.6g

Ingredients

- ❖ 60 ml (1/4 cup) thickened cream
- ❖ 2 x 180 g good-quality white chocolate, finely chopped
- ❖ 2 tsp Malibu liqueur

Directions

1. In a microwave-safe bowl, heat the thickened cream in the microwave for 35 seconds on high.
2. Add the finely chopped white chocolate to the bowl and stir until the chocolate is fully melted and smooth.
3. Stir in the Malibu liqueur until well combined.
4. Cover the bowl with plastic wrap and refrigerate for at least 30 minutes or until the mixture is firm enough to roll into balls.
5. Once the mixture has chilled, roll them into small balls.
6. Place the rolled truffles on a plate lined with parchment paper and chill in the refrigerator for an additional 15-20 minutes until they are firm.
7. Once the truffles have firmed up, you can decorate them with nuts, sprinkles and other toppings.

Béchamel Sauce

Servings 8 | Time| 15 minutes

Nutritional Content

Cal 57 | Fat 4 g | Protein 1.7 g | Carbs 3.7 g| Fiber | 0.1g

Ingredients

- ❖ 360 ml (1 1/2 cups) warm milk
- ❖ 30 g (2 tbsp.) butter
- ❖ 30 g (2 tbsp.) plain flour

Directions

1. In a microwave-safe container, melt the butter for 30 seconds at HIGH (100%) power.
2. Add the flour and stir until combined. Microwave for 30 seconds at HIGH power.
3. Gradually add the warm milk, stirring constantly to avoid lumps. Microwave for 1 minute at HIGH power.
4. Stir the sauce well and microwave for another 1 minute at HIGH power.
5. Repeat step 4 until the sauce thickens, stirring every minute. This can take 3-5 minutes, depending on the power of your microwave.
6. Season with salt and pepper to taste and stir well.
7. Transfer the sauce to a heatproof bowl and cover with plastic wrap, pressing it onto the surface of the sauce to prevent a skin from forming.
8. Allow the sauce to cool before storing in the fridge for up to 4 days.

Note: Bechamel sauce can sometimes form lumps when made in the microwave. To prevent this, whisk the sauce vigorously after each microwave interval. If you do end up with lumps, strain the sauce through a fine-mesh strainer to remove them

Pears Crisp

Servings 2 | Time| 10 minutes

Nutritional Content

Cal 540 | Fat 31.5 g | Protein 4.5 g | Carbs 67 g| Fiber | 8.5g

Ingredients

- ❖ 45 ml (3 tablespoons) coconut oil
- ❖ 10 g (1/4 cup) quick oats
- ❖ 30 g (2 tablespoons) chopped walnuts
- ❖ 40 g (2 1/2 tablespoons) whole wheat flour (divided)
- ❖ 40 g (2 1/2 tablespoons) sugar (divided)
- ❖ 2 g (1/2 teaspoon) cinnamon (divided)
- ❖ ½ g (1/8 teaspoon) salt
- ❖ 2–3 pears (about 2 cups chopped)
- ❖ Honey for drizzling

Directions

1. Melt the coconut oil in the microwave. Add salt, 1/4 teaspoon cinnamon, 2 tablespoons sugar, 2 tablespoons whole wheat flour, oats, and walnuts. Mix thoroughly after combining.
2. Chop the pears and mix with 1/4 teaspoon cinnamon, 1/2 tablespoon sugar, and 1/2 tablespoon whole wheat flour.
3. Spoon a little of the oat mixture into two ramekins or cups. Add about 1 cup of diced pears on top and then sprinkle the remaining oat mixture. Microwave for 3 minutes and 30 seconds.
4. The dish will shrink, and the pears will bubble. Let it cool before serving, and drizzle honey on top for a gooey texture.

Microwave Sweet Potato Chips

Servings 8 | Time| 15 minutes

Nutritional Content

Cal 46 | Fat 0.2 g | Protein 1 g | Carbs 10.5 g| Fiber | 1.6g

Ingredients

- ❖ Cooking spray
- ❖ 400 g (1 (14-ounce)) sweet potato, very thinly sliced, divided
- ❖ 5 g (1 teaspoon) finely chopped fresh thyme, divided
- ❖ 2 g (1/2 teaspoon) salt, divided
- ❖ 1 g (1/4 teaspoon) freshly ground black pepper, divided

Directions

1. To fit a microwave-safe plate, cut a circle of parchment paper and lightly spray it with cooking spray.
2. Place 250 grams of potato slices on parchment in a single layer. Sprinkle 1 gram of thyme, 0.5 grams of salt, and a pinch of pepper evenly.
3. Microwave for 4 minutes at POWER LEVEL 9.
4. Check for doneness.
5. Cook for an additional 30 seconds at a time until finished.
6. Repeat with the remaining potato, rosemary, salt, and pepper in the same way.
7. All measurements are in grams and millilitres, and all sizes are in centimetres.

Microwave Egg Sandwich

Servings 1| Time| 60 minutes

Nutritional Content

Cal 405 | Fat 22.5 g | Protein 22.9 g | Carbs 32.7 g| Fiber | 7.6g

Ingredients

- ❖ 2 large eggs
- ❖ ½ g (1/8 teaspoon) kosher salt
- ❖ Pinch of fresh ground black pepper
- ❖ 30 g (2 tablespoons) grated cheddar
- ❖ 1 English muffin
- ❖ 1/4 avocado, sliced

Directions

1. Spray the bowl with non-stick cooking spray or a small layer of oil or butter. Use a fork to mix the eggs, salt, pepper, and 1 Tbsp. of water.
2. After 30 seconds on high in the microwave, you should see solid pieces of egg floating in the uncooked part.
3. Stir the egg carefully to help it cook more evenly. Microwave the egg for another 30 seconds, or until it puffs up noticeably.
4. Add cheese and microwave for an additional 15 to 30 seconds, or until just set. Use a small spatula to transfer the egg mixture to the bottom slice of toast.
5. Place avocado on top, followed by hot sauce or pesto, and the final slice of toast. Serve immediately.

DESSERT RECIPES

Microwave Sunflower seeds Brittle

Servings 36 | Time| 30 minutes

Nutritional Content

Cal 42 | Fat 0.6 g | Protein 0.3 g | Carbs 9.1 g| Fiber | 0.1 g

Ingredients

- 220 g (1 cup) white sugar
- 155 ml (1/2 cup) light maple syrup
- 145 g (1 cup) Sunflower seeds

- 5 g (1 teaspoon) butter
- 5 g (1 teaspoon) vanilla extract
- 5 g (1 teaspoon) baking soda

Directions

1. Use butter to grease your cookie sheet.
2. Sugar and maple syrup should be combined in a 2-quart glass basin. on high for 4 minutes in the microwave.
3. Add the sunflower seed, stir, and microwave for an additional 3 1/2 minutes on high. Add vanilla and butter and stir. For one minute and thirty seconds, microwave.
4. Baking soda should be added and stirred until the batter is bright and frothy. Onto the baking sheet, pour the batter. Spread it thinly and evenly.
5. Cool thoroughly before breaking.
6. Enjoy!

Microwave Almond Butter Fudge

Servings 64 | Time| 05 minutes

Nutritional Content

Cal 77 | Fat 4.9 g | Protein 1 g | Carbs 7.9g| Fiber | 0.2 g

Ingredients

- ❖ 225 g (8 oz) unsalted butter
- ❖ 260 g (1 cup) almond butter
- ❖ 450 g (1 pound) powdered sugar

Directions

1. Start by lining a 20 cm x 20 cm pan with parchment paper, making sure to leave enough hanging over the sides. This will make it easier to remove the fudge from the pan.
2. Combine the butter and almond butter in a microwave-safe bowl and microwave for one minute. Stir the mixture until smooth, then microwave for an additional minute while continuing to stir.
3. Once the mixture is smooth, add the powdered sugar and stir until the batter becomes thick and paste-like.
4. Spread the batter evenly on the lined baking pan and use a layer of parchment paper to press it down with your palms.
5. Place the pan in the fridge for at least two hours. Once it has set, remove the fudge from the pan using a sharp knife and cut it into small 1-inch squares.
6. Enjoy your delicious fudge!

Salted Caramel Fudge

Servings 16 | Time| 40 minutes

Nutritional Content

Cal 231 | Fat 14.6 g | Protein 3 g | Carbs 22.8 g| Fiber | 0 g

Ingredients

- ❖ 150 g (1 cup) unsalted butter
- ❖ 400 ml (1-1/2 cups) sweetened condensed milk
- ❖ 500 g brown sugar
- ❖ Good pinch of sea salt (plus extra for sprinkling)
- ❖ 250 g (1 cup) white chocolate

Directions

1. Grease and line an 18 cm x 28 cm rectangular slice pan with parchment paper before using it.
2. Place the butter, condensed milk, and brown sugar in a microwave-safe bowl. Heat the mixture in the microwave for 8 minutes, stirring every 2 minutes until melted.
3. Stir in sea salt until the white chocolate is melted.
4. Sprinkle more sea salt on top of the fudge after pouring it into the prepared tin.
5. Chill the dish in the refrigerator for 2 hours to set before cutting it into pieces.

Microwave Christmas Fudge

Servings 16 | Time| 2 hr.5 minutes

Nutritional Content

Cal 279 | Fat 14.6 g | Protein 4.9 g | Carbs 35.5 g| Fiber | 0.6 g

Ingredients

- ❖ 500 g (2 cups) white chocolate
- ❖ 400 ml (1-1/2 cups) sweetened condensed milk
- ❖ 80 g (3/4 cup) pistachios chopped
- ❖ 150 g (1-1/2 cups) dried cranberries (craisins)

Directions

1. Prepare a 20 cm x 20 cm square baking pan by greasing it and lining it with parchment paper.
2. Combine the white chocolate melts and sweetened condensed milk in a microwave-safe bowl. Melt in the microwave for 2-3 minutes, stirring every minute until completely melted.
3. Stir in the chopped pistachios and dried cranberries, reserving some for later.
4. Sprinkle the remaining pistachios and cranberries over the top and press down lightly.
5. Refrigerate the dish for 2 hours to set before cutting into pieces.

Microwave Rocky Road Fudge

Servings 20 | Time| 15 minutes

Nutritional Content

Cal 226 | Fat 11.6 g | Protein 3.1 g | Carbs 27.5 g| Fiber | 1.9 g

Ingredients

- ❖ 340 g (2 cups) semisweet chocolate chips
- ❖ 400 g (1 14-ounce can) sweetened condensed milk
- ❖ 2 g (1/2 teaspoon) vanilla extract

- ❖ 150 g (2 1/2 cups) miniature marshmallows
- ❖ 150 g (1 cup) chopped walnuts
- ❖ cooking spray

Directions

1. Prepare a pan by lining it with foil and spraying it with cooking spray.
2. In a microwave-safe bowl, mix the chocolate chips and condensed milk. Melt in 45-second intervals in the microwave. Stir in vanilla extract until smooth.
3. Add the marshmallows and nuts and mix gently.
4. Pour the mixture into the prepared pan and refrigerate until ready to serve. To serve, remove the fudge from the pan using the foil and slice into bite-sized pieces.

Fantasy Fudge

Servings 40 | Time| 10 minutes

Nutritional Content

Cal 170 | Fat 8 g | Protein 1.1 g | Carbs 25 g| Fiber | 0.7 g

Ingredients

- ❖ 660 g (3 cups) white sugar
- ❖ 170 g (3/4 cup) margarine
- ❖ 160 ml (2/3 cup) evaporated milk
- ❖ 340 g (1 (12 oz)) package semisweet chocolate chips
- ❖ 200 g (1 (7 oz)) jar marshmallow creme
- ❖ 170 g (1 cup) chopped walnuts
- ❖ 5 g (1 teaspoon) vanilla extract

Directions

1. Prepare a regular sized baking pan by greasing it.
2. Place margarine in a microwave-safe dish and heat until melted. Blend in milk and sugar.
3. Microwave mixture on high for 5 minutes, stirring after 3 minutes and scraping the sides of the bowl. Microwave for an additional 5 and a half minutes.
4. Remove from the microwave and add chocolate chips, vanilla extract, walnuts, and marshmallow creme. Mix well.
5. Pour mixture into prepared pan and let it cool. Cut into squares.
6. Enjoy!

Turtles

Servings 12 | Time| 15 minutes

Nutritional Content

Cal 808 | Fat 49.6 g | Protein 8.9 g | Carbs 86.5 g| Fiber | 6.1 g

Ingredients

- ❖ 50 pecan halves (get a little extra in case some break)
- ❖ 30 individually wrapped caramels
- ❖ 15 g (1 tablespoon) heavy cream
- ❖ 210 g (1 1/4 cups) semi-sweet chocolate chips
- ❖ 5 ml (1 teaspoon) coconut oil (optional)

Directions

1. Spread parchment paper over a sizable cookie sheet.
2. Pecans should be arranged into twelve Xs, each with four protruding legs.
3. Caramels should be unwrapped and put in a microwave-safe bowl. Use a basin that is not too small. You must be able to stir it with ease. Add cream, then cook for 30 seconds at 50% power. Heat for 15 second intervals at 50% power if not melting. Between each interval, stir. One heaping tablespoon is placed in the middle of each batch of pecans after stirring. Allow the caramel to cool for at least 15 to 20 minutes at room temperature.
4. Coconut oil and chocolate chips should be melted in the microwave for one minute on 50% power. Stir until the basin is no longer warm to the touch. until completely melted, keep heating at 50% power for intervals of 15 to 30 seconds. Up until the bowl no longer feels warm, stir continuously.
5. With the back of the spoon, spread and swirl chocolate over the caramel. For many hours, let the candies sit at room temperature.

Pumpkin Cake

Servings 1| Time| 05 minutes

Nutritional Content

Cal 214 | Fat 1.6 g | Protein 5.9 g | Carbs 44.9 g| Fiber | 2.9 g

Ingredients

- ❖ 30 g (4 tbsp) plain flour
- ❖ 10 g (2 tbsp) white sugar
- ❖ 4 g (1 tsp) baking powder
- ❖ 2 g (½ tsp) cinnamon
- ❖ 1 g (¼ tsp) nutmeg
- ❖ pinch of ground clove

- ❖ 1 g (¼ tsp) ground ginger
- ❖ pinch salt
- ❖ 30 g (2 tbsp) pumpkin puree
- ❖ 2 g (½ tsp) vanilla extract
- ❖ 45 ml (3 tbsp) milk

Directions

1. In a 340 g (12 oz) mug, combine all dry ingredients.
2. Add the milk, vanilla, and pumpkin puree.
3. To prevent dry particles from getting caught at the bottom, thoroughly combine, paying careful attention to the bottom.
4. 2 minutes on high in the microwave.
5. If desired, garnish with whipped cream and cinnamon.

Lemon cake

Servings 1 | Time| 05 minutes

Nutritional Content

Cal 395 | Fat 14.2 g | Protein 5.9 g | Carbs 66.3 g| Fiber 2.7 g

Ingredients

- ❖ 30 g (4 tbsp.) almond flour
- ❖ 1 g (1/4 tsp) baking powder
- ❖ 45 ml (3 tbsp.) almond milk
- ❖ 10 g (2 1/2 tbsp.) coconut sugar

- ❖ 15 ml (1 tbsp.) vegetable oil
- ❖ 15 ml (1 tbsp.) fresh squeezed lemon juice
- ❖ lemon zest

Directions

1. In a cup that can be used in a microwave, whisk together the flour, baking powder, sugar, milk, oil, and lemon juice until the batter is smooth.
2. Add some freshly grated lemon zest to the batter and mix it in.
3. Cook for roughly one minute in the microwave.
4. Cake should have a dry top. Before eating, allow to cool.
5. If desired, add a lemon glaze.

Churro

Servings 1 | Time| 15 minutes

Nutritional Content

Cal 350 | Fat 15.3 g | Protein 4.8 g | Carbs 51.6 g| Fiber | 1.9 g

Ingredients

- ❖ 30 g (4 tablespoons) coconut flour
- ❖ 10 g (2 tablespoons) sugar
- ❖ ½ g (⅛ teaspoon) baking powder
- ❖ 1 g (1/16 teaspoon) baking soda
- ❖ 1 g (¼ teaspoon) cinnamon
- ❖ 45 ml (3 tablespoons) milk
- ❖ 15 ml (1 tablespoon) vegetable oil
- ❖ 15 g (1 tablespoons) roughly chopped chocolate

Directions

1. In a microwave-safe cup, combine flour, baking powder, baking soda, sugar, and cinnamon.
2. Pour in the milk and vegetable oil, then stir until a smooth batter forms. Don't worry about a few lumps.
3. Place a spoonful of chopped chocolate into the center of the batter.
4. Microwave the cake for 45 to 60 seconds, or until it has risen and feels firm to the touch. Adjust the timing to suit your microwave's wattage.
5. Sprinkle the remaining combined cinnamon and sugar over the cake, then enjoy immediately.

Blondie

Servings 1 | Time| 11 minutes

Nutritional Content

Cal 718 | Fat 31.1 g | Protein 9 g | Carbs 102.5 g| Fiber | 1.9 g

Ingredients

- ❖ 30 g (2 tablespoons) butter, melted
- ❖ 35 (3 tablespoons) brown sugar
- ❖ 45 ml (3 tablespoons) milk
- ❖ 2 g (½ teaspoon) vanilla
- ❖ 50 g (6 tablespoons) flour
- ❖ ½ g (1/8 teaspoon) salt
- ❖ ½ g (1/8 teaspoon) baking powder
- ❖ 15 g (1 tablespoon) white chocolate chips
- ❖ 4 caramel candies, chopped
- ❖ Ice cream and caramel sauce for topping (optional)

Directions

1. Melt butter in a large, microwave-safe mug.
2. Add brown sugar, milk, and vanilla. Stir until sugar dissolves.
3. Gradually add flour, salt, and baking powder. Mix well.
4. Add caramel candies and white chocolate chips. Cover and refrigerate for up to two days. Microwave for 1 minute and 20 seconds when ready to eat. Microwave for an additional 30 seconds if undercooked.
5. Top with ice cream and caramel sauce, then enjoy!

Peanut Butter Cup

Servings 1 | Time| 05 minutes

Nutritional Content

Cal 439 | Fat 28.6 g | Protein 10.9 g | Carbs 41.5 g| Fiber | 2.9 g

Ingredients

- ❖ 10 g (1/2 Tbsp.) butter
- ❖ 35 g (2 Tbsp.) creamy peanut butter
- ❖ 5 g (2 tsp.) powdered sugar
- ❖ 35 g (5 Tbsp.) crushed graham crackers
- ❖ 30 g (2 Tbsp.) dark chocolate chips

Directions

1. Combine butter and peanut butter in a microwave-safe mug. Microwave for 30 seconds.
2. Thoroughly mix graham cracker crumbs and powdered sugar.
3. Sprinkle chocolate chips on top and microwave for 45 seconds. Spread the melted chocolate over the peanut butter.
4. Enjoy!

Oreo Mug Cake

Servings 1 | Time| 05 minutes

Nutritional Content

Cal 595 | Fat 25.6 g | Protein 11.9 g | Carbs 85.5 g| Fiber | 4.9 g

Ingredients

- ❖ 90 ml (6 tbsp.) coconut milk
- ❖ 15 ml (1 tbsp.) olive oil
- ❖ 30 g (1/4 cup) coconut flour
- ❖ 30 g (2 tbsp.) unsweetened cocoa powder
- ❖ 10 g (2 tbsp.) coconut sugar
- ❖ 2 Oreos lightly crushed,
- ❖ 1 g (1/4 tsp) baking powder
- ❖ 1 pinch salt
- ❖ 15 g (1 tbsp.) dark chocolate

Directions

1. In a large cup, whisk together coconut milk and olive oil.
2. Combine coconut flour, unsweetened cocoa powder, crushed Oreos, coconut sugar, baking soda, and salt in a small bowl.
3. Add the flour mixture to the cup and stir thoroughly to remove any lumps.
4. If desired, top with additional crumbled Oreos and chocolate.
5. Place the mixture on a microwave-safe dish and cook for 1 minute 20 seconds. Allow it to cool before enjoying!

Red Velvet Microwave Cake

Servings 1 | Time| 10 minutes

Nutritional Content

Cal 790 | Fat 46 g | Protein 11.9 g | Carbs 85.5 g| Fiber | 3.9 g

Ingredients

- 30 g (4 tablespoons) flour
- 30 g (4 1/2 tablespoons) sugar
- ½ g (1/8 teaspoon) baking powder
- 10 g (1 1/2 tablespoons) unsweetened cocoa powder
- pinch of salt
- pinch of cinnamon
- 45 ml (3 tablespoons) oil

- 45 ml (3 tablespoons) buttermilk (substitute sour cream or yogurt if not available)
- 1 egg
- 4 g (1 teaspoon) Vanilla extract
- 2 g (1/2 teaspoons) red food colouring

Directions

1. Stir all the wet ingredients with a fork in a large mug until the batter is smooth.
2. Add the dry ingredients and mix them in.
3. Microwave the cake for 50 seconds, but cooking time may vary for different microwaves.
4. Be careful not to overcook, as this can cause the cake to become dense and rubbery.
5. Allow the cake to cool before adding the cream cheese icing.

Bread Pudding

Servings 1 | Time| 10 minutes

Nutritional Content

Cal 910 | Fat 36 g | Protein 21.9 g | Carbs 107.5 g| Fiber | 0 g

Ingredients

- ❖ Sweet Rolls cubed
- ❖ 30 g (2 tablespoons) chocolate chips
- ❖ 1 egg
- ❖ 10 g (2 tablespoons) sugar

- ❖ 80 ml (⅓ cup) milk
- ❖ ½ g (⅛ teaspoon) cinnamon
- ❖ 1 g (¼ teaspoon) vanilla
- ❖ Sprinkle of nutmeg

Directions

1. Cut two rolls in half and butter both sides.
2. Make four cubes out of each side.
3. Combine egg, sugar, milk, cinnamon, and vanilla in a small bowl.
4. Put chocolate chips and buttered cubes in a large microwave-safe ramekin.
5. Pour egg mixture over the bread and press it in with a fork or fingers to ensure full coverage.
6. Sprinkle nutmeg on top.
7. After microwaving for 1 minute, check to make sure there is no large egg pool in the bottom by pulling bread away from the sides with a fork. Check the middle too.
8. Microwave for an additional 30 seconds and repeat the inspection.
9. Continue microwaving at 15-second intervals until the egg mixture is set.

Mocha Microwave Cake

Servings 1 | Time| 10 minutes

Nutritional Content

Cal 522 | Fat 24.6 g | Protein 7.9 g | Carbs 71.5 g| Fiber | 3.9 g

Ingredients

- ❖ 75 ml (5 tablespoons) brewed coffee, divided
- ❖ 45 g (3 tablespoons) chocolate chips
- ❖ 35 g (¼ cup) almond flour
- ❖ 30 g (2 tablespoons) granulated sugar
- ❖ 5g (1 tablespoon) cocoa powder
- ❖ 1 g (¼ teaspoon) baking powder
- ❖ pinch of salt
- ❖ 30 ml (2 tablespoons) milk
- ❖ 15 ml (1 tablespoon) vegetable oil

Directions

1. Place chocolate chips and 3 tablespoons (45 ml) of coffee in a sizable, microwave-safe mug. Stir until smooth. If coffee is cold, heat in mug for 10 seconds on high, stirring to achieve smooth consistency. Microwave for additional 10 seconds if needed.
2. Combine flour, sugar, baking powder, salt, and cocoa powder in a small bowl.
3. Add dry ingredients, milk, remaining 2 tablespoons of coffee, and oil. Whisk until combined, avoiding overmixing.
4. Pour cake batter into mug over chocolate and coffee mixture.
5. Cover mug with folded paper towel and microwave on high for 90 seconds. Check top for wet batter. Microwave in 10-second intervals until cake is fully cooked, checking after each interval.

Pumpkin Cornbread Mug Cake

Servings 1 | Time| 10 minutes

Nutritional Content

Cal 235 | Fat 1.6 g | Protein 6 g | Carbs 51 g| Fiber | 7.2 g

Ingredients

- 45 g (3 tbsp.) coconut Flour
- 30 g (2 tbsp.) Yellow Cornmeal
- 2 g (½ Tsp) Baking Powder
- 1 g (¼ Tsp) Baking Soda
- 2 g (½ Tsp) Cinnamon
- 1 g (¼ Tsp) Vanilla Extract
- 8 Drops Liquid Vanilla Stevia
- 45 g (3 tbsp.) Pure Pumpkin Puree
- 45 ml (3 tbsp.) Water

Directions

1. Combine the first five dry ingredients in a small mug. Add the next four wet ingredients and mix well.
2. Heat the ramekin on high for 1 minute and 20-30 seconds. Be careful when taking it out as it will be hot. Top with your choice and enjoy!

Banana Chocolate Chip Minute Muffins

Servings 1 | Time| 05 minutes

Nutritional Content

Cal 466 | Fat 9.1 g | Protein 5.9 g | Carbs 95.5 g| Fiber | 4.5 g

Ingredients

- 45 g (3 tbsp.) biscuit mix
- ½ of a banana mashed
- 10 g (2 tbsp.) instant oatmeal
- 15 ml (1 tbsp.) milk
- 15 ml (1 tbsp.)
- 15 ml (1 tbsp.) mini chocolate chips
- 30 g (2-3 tbsp.) honey

Directions

1. Put the ingredients in a cup or microwave-safe mug.
2. Microwave on high power for one minute.
3. Let it cool and use a spoon to enjoy.
4. Optionally, add honey as a topping.

Chocolate Mug Cake

Servings 2 | Time| 15 minutes

Nutritional Content

Cal 523 | Fat 23.6 g | Protein 6.1 g | Carbs 80.5 g| Fiber | 4.4 g

Ingredients

- ❖ 60 g (1/2 cup) coconut flour
- ❖ 100 g (1/2 cup) sugar
- ❖ 60 g (4 tbsp.) unsweetened Cocoa
- ❖ 45 ml (3 tbsp.) whole milk
- ❖ 45 ml (3 tbsp.) Canola oil
- ❖ 1 g (1/4 tsp.) Pure vanilla extract

Directions

1. Combine all ingredients in a bowl and stir.
2. Pour mixture into two mugs.
3. Microwave on high for 1 1/2 minutes.
4. If needed, cook for an additional 30 seconds to 1 minute.
5. Allow to cool for 2 minutes.
6. Top with desired toppings such as icing, whipped cream, chocolate chips, chocolate syrup, or a drizzle of heavy whipping cream.

Brownie

Servings 1 | Time| 05 minutes

Nutritional Content

Cal 514 | Fat 28.6 g | Protein 7.2 g | Carbs 60.5 g| Fiber | 2.6 g

Ingredients

- ❖ 30 g (2 Tablespoons) Butter
- ❖ 10 g (2 Tablespoons) White Sugar
- ❖ 5 g (1 Tablespoon) Brown Sugar Packed
- ❖ 2 g (½ Teaspoon) Vanilla Extract
- ❖ 1 Egg Yolk
- ❖ 30 g (4 Tablespoons) plain Flour
- ❖ 15 g (1 Tablespoon) Unsweetened Cocoa Powder
- ❖ 60 g (4 Tablespoons) Chocolate Chunks
- ❖ Pinch of Salt to Taste

Directions

1. Microwave butter in a safe cup for 20-30 seconds.
2. Mix in salt, vanilla, brown sugar, white sugar, and egg yolk.
3. Stir in flour and chocolate powder, avoiding overmixing.
4. Fold in chocolate pieces.
5. Cook for 45-60 seconds, being careful not to overcook as the mixture will stiffen up when it cools.

Kale ricotta Lasagne

Servings 1 | Time| 15 minutes

Nutritional Content

Cal 249 | Fat 9.6 g | Protein 14.3 g | Carbs 27.1 g| Fiber | 4.8 g

Ingredients

- ❖ 10 g (1/2) fresh lasagne sheet
- ❖ 75 g (2 1/2 cups) baby kale, roughly chopped
- ❖ 1/4 medium pepper,
- ❖ 30 g (1/4 cup) part-skim ricotta cheese
- ❖ 3 large thyme leaves, finely chopped (optional)
- ❖ 1 g (1/4 tsp) kosher salt
- ❖ ½ g (1/8 tsp) garlic
- ❖ 90 g (6 tbsp.) ketchup
- ❖ 10 g (1/3 cup) mozzarella

Directions

1. Cut each lasagna strip in half and then again. Place pasta sheets in a bowl and cover with extremely hot water. Keep pasta pieces separated.
2. Microwave chopped spinach in a microwave-safe bowl with plastic wrap and ventilation holes for 1 minute. Set aside to cool.
3. Grate the mozzarella while waiting for the spinach to cool.
4. Combine ricotta, salt, pepper, and minced garlic with the cooled spinach. Separate the mixture.
5. Add 2 tablespoons of pasta sauce to the bottom of a mug. Add a softened pasta sheet, spinach mixture, and 2 tablespoons of mozzarella. Continue layering, ending with a pasta sheet on top. Add mozzarella on top of the noodles.
6. Microwave for 1 minute and 30 seconds. Check if mozzarella is melted. If not, microwave in 15-second increments until melted.
7. Serve immediately.

Spiced Lentils

Servings 1 | Time| 05 minutes

Nutritional Content

Cal 240 | Fat 1.6 g | Protein 16g | Carbs 41 g| Fiber | 13 g

Ingredients

- ❖ 150 g (3/4 cup) rinsed drained canned lentils
- ❖ 280 ml (1/2 can (10 oz)) reduced sodium diced tomatoes w/ green chiles (e.g., Ro-Tel), undrained
- ❖ 2 g (1/2 tsp) ground cumin
- ❖ 1 g (1/4 tsp) ground ginger

- ❖ ½ g (1/8 tsp) hot pepper sauce
- ❖ 15 g (1 tbsp.) plain Greek yogurt
- ❖ 15 g (1 tbsp.) chopped roasted salted almonds
- ❖ 10 g (2 tsp) chopped fresh mint

Directions

1. In a large mug, mix lentils, tomatoes, cumin, ginger, and spicy sauce.
2. Microwave on high for 1 1/2 to 2 1/2 minutes until hot.
3. Add yoghurt on top and sprinkle with mint and almonds.
4. Serve with warm naan if desired.
5. Enjoy!

Easy Mac

Servings 1 | Time| 05 minutes

Nutritional Content

Cal 375 | Fat 24.6 g | Protein 13.2 g | Carbs 27 g| Fiber | 1.3 g

Ingredients

- ❖ 40 g (1/3 cup) Pasta
- ❖ 120 ml (1/2 cup) Water
- ❖ 1 pinch Salt

- ❖ 60 ml (1/4 cup) milk
- ❖ 30 g (1/4 cup) Shredded cheese

Directions

1. Mix pasta noodles, water, and salt in a large mug. Microwave for 2 minutes, remove and stir. Repeat twice more for a total of 6 minutes.
2. Pasta should be al dente and water almost absorbed.
3. Add milk and cheese. Microwave for 2 more minutes, stirring every 30 seconds until cheese is melted.
4. Stir once more after removing from microwave, then season to taste.
5. Mix everything together and enjoy!

Cheesy Spinach Microwave Scrambled Eggs Mug

Servings 1 | Time| 03 minutes

Nutritional Content

Cal 289 | Fat 21 g | Protein 22.8 g | Carbs 2.4 g| Fiber | 0.2 g

Ingredients

- ❖ 3 large eggs
- ❖ 30 ml (2 tablespoons) water,
- ❖ 8 g (¼ cup) baby spinach
- ❖ salt and pepper to taste
- ❖ 30 g (2 tablespoons) shredded cheese

Directions

1. Before cooking, spray a large mug with non-stick cooking spray, taking into account that the eggs will rise.
2. Crack the eggs into the mug and mix in water, milk, or cream, as well as salt and pepper. Stir thoroughly.
3. Stir in spinach. If the leaves are too large, use your fingers to tear them apart slightly.
4. Cooking time in the microwave will vary. Microwave the eggs on high for 30 seconds, stir, and then microwave for an additional 30 seconds. Once the eggs are fully cooked and the cheese has melted, stir and sprinkle cheese on top. Microwave for an additional 15 to 45 seconds.
5. The eggs will be hot, but if necessary, transfer them to a platter or eat straight from the mug.

Avocado macaroni

Servings 2 | Time| 05 minutes

Nutritional Content

Cal 486 | Fat 29.2 g | Protein 20.5 g | Carbs 36.4 g| Fiber | 4.7 g

Ingredients

- ❖ 105 g (1 cup) elbow macaroni
- ❖ 240 ml (1 cup) water
- ❖ 115 g (1 cup) shredded cheddar cheese
- ❖ 1/2 of a ripe avocado
- ❖ salt and pepper to taste

Directions

1. Fill a large mug with water and pasta.
2. Put the mug on a dish to catch any overflow.
3. Stir after each minute in the microwave to prevent sticking. After three minutes, the noodles should be almost done.
4. Add an extra 30 seconds if needed.
5. While the macaroni is cooking, mash the avocado into small pieces with a spoon.
6. Drain any remaining water from the mug. Add cheese and stir until covered. Microwave for 20 seconds more if needed.
7. Combine with mashed avocado, then add salt and pepper to taste.
8. Eat immediately.

Broccoli and Cheese Rice Bowl

Servings 1 | Time| 10 minutes

Nutritional Content

Cal 350 | Fat 3.6 g | Protein 15.1 g | Carbs 56.3 g| Fiber | 3.1 g

Ingredients

- ❖ 60 g (5 tablespoons) rice (quick cooking)
- ❖ 150 g (⅔ cup) cold water
- ❖ 2 broccoli florets (finely chopped)
- ❖ 2 g (½ teaspoon) corn flour
- ❖ 45 ml (3 tablespoons) milk
- ❖ 60 g (4 tablespoons) grated cheddar
- ❖ Salt to taste

Directions

1. Rice, broccoli, and cold water should all be combined in a mug. A plate should be placed on top of the mug. The fastest method of cooking is a rapid cooking.
2. for 3 1/2 to 4 minutes on high. Keep a tight check on it as it cooks because if the mug is too small, the water may overflow.
3. Remove the rice from the microwave once it has finished cooking, then stir in the milk, cornflour, cheese that has been granted, and a little salt.
4. Reheat the mixture for 1 minute 30 seconds by placing it back in the microwave.

Pizza in a mug

Servings 36 | Time| 30 minutes

Nutritional Content

Cal 671 | Fat 55.6 g | Protein 33 g | Carbs 14.3 g| Fiber | 3.6 g

Ingredients

- ❖ 15 g (1 Tablespoon) butter, melted
- ❖ 1 egg yolk
- ❖ 10 g (1/4 Cup) Almond Flour
- ❖ 2 g (1/2 Teaspoon) baking powder
- ❖ 2 g (1/2 Teaspoon) Italian seasoning
- ❖ Sprinkle of garlic powder
- ❖ Sprinkle of onion powder
- ❖ 30 ml (2 Tablespoons) unsweetened almond milk
- ❖ 30 g (2 Tablespoons) shredded mozzarella cheese
- ❖ 6-8 pepperoni slices, chopped

Directions

1. In a large mug or big microwaveable ramekin, melt 1 Tablespoon of butter.
2. Microwave the remaining ingredients for 1 minute and 30 seconds on high (I have a 1000-watt microwave - you may need to adjust times slightly for higher or lower wattage).

Brown Rice with Edamame and Pineapple

Servings 36 | Time| 30 minutes

Nutritional Content

Cal 269 | Fat 6.5 g | Protein 8 g | Carbs 45.3 g| Fiber | 2.9 g

Ingredients

- ❖ 110 g (1/2 cup) instant brown rice
- ❖ 150 ml (2/3 cup) water
- ❖ 80 g (1/3 cup) frozen shelled edamame
- ❖ 50 g (1/4 cup) diced fresh or drained canned pineapple
- ❖ 10 ml (1 tablespoon) teriyaki sauce
- ❖ 20 g (2 tablespoons) chopped cashews
- ❖ Optional Hot pepper sauce (sliced green onions, chopped fresh mint, cilantro)

Directions

1. Combine rice and water in a mug.
2. Add edamame on top.
3. Place a small dish or sauce on top and microwave on high for 5 to 6 minutes until water is absorbed.
4. Remove from microwave, cover for 1 minute, and let rest to absorb remaining moisture.
5. Stir in pineapple and teriyaki sauce.
6. Microwave pineapple uncovered for 30 to 45 seconds until warm.
7. Let it stand for a minute, stir, then add hot pepper sauce to taste.
8. Add cashews and any other desired ingredients.

Fettuccine Alfredo in a Mug

Servings 1 | Time| 15 minutes

Nutritional Content

Cal 516 | Fat 33.6 g | Protein 21.7 g | Carbs 34.1 g| Fiber | 0.1 g

Ingredients

- ❖ 55 g (2 oz) Fettuccine pasta, cooked
- ❖ 15 g (1 tablespoon) butter
- ❖ 60 g (1/4 cup) heavy cream
- ❖ 45 g (3 tablespoons) grated cheese
- ❖ 1 g (1/4 teaspoon) garlic powder
- ❖ Salt and pepper to taste

Directions

1. Put all the ingredients into a microwaveable mug that is medium sized.
2. Microwave the mug on high for 1 1/2 minutes. You will see that the sauce has thickened once everything is mixed.
3. Add extra cheese on top and savour!
4. To create a less heavy dessert, combine it with my microwave mug sponge cake.

Kale Ricotta Lasagne in a Mug

Servings 1 | Time| 15 minutes

Nutritional Content

Cal 242 | Fat 9.6 g | Protein 14.6 g | Carbs 27 g| Fiber | 4.6 g

Ingredients

- ❖ 1/2 fresh lasagne sheet
- ❖ 75 g (2 1/2 cups) baby kale, roughly chopped
- ❖ 1/4 medium yellow bell pepper, diced
- ❖ 30 g (1/4 cup) part-skim ricotta cheese
- ❖ 3 large basil leaves, finely chopped (optional)

- ❖ 1 g (1/4 tsp) kosher salt
- ❖ ½ g (1/8 tsp) granulated garlic
- ❖ 90 g (6 tbsp.) pasta sauce or tomato sauce
- ❖ 10 g (1/3 cup) shredded part-skim mozzarella

Directions

1. Cut each lasagne strip into four pieces. Place the pasta in a bowl and cover with hot water from an electric kettle. Keep them separate.
2. Microwave chopped kale in a vented bowl for one minute. Set aside to cool.
3. Grate the mozzarella while waiting.
4. Mix the spinach with ricotta, salt, pepper, and garlic. Separate the mixture.
5. In a mug, add 2 tbsp of pasta sauce to the bottom. Layer with pasta, kale, and mozzarella. Repeat and top with a pasta sheet and more mozzarella.
6. Microwave for 1 minute and 30 seconds until the cheese is melted. Microwave in 15-second increments if needed.
7. Serve immediately.

Omelette in a Mug

Servings 1 | Time| 10 minutes

Nutritional Content

Cal 349 | Fat 12.4 g | Protein 33 g | Carbs 27.4 g| Fiber | 3.8 g

Ingredients

- ❖ 2 large eggs
- ❖ 10 g (1 tbsp.) flour
- ❖ 15 ml (1 tbsp.) skim milk
- ❖ 15 g (1 tbsp.) low-fat grated cheese
- ❖ 20 g (2 tbsp.) diced green pepper
- ❖ 20 g (2 tbsp.) diced onion
- ❖ 70 g (½ a Perfect cooked Boneless Skinless Chicken Breast fillet
- ❖ Salt/pepper

Directions

1. Begin by cracking and beating your eggs in a small bowl or your mug.
2. Add the milk, cheese, flour, and diced vegetables to the egg mixture after stirring.
3. Cut the chicken breast in half, then into tiny pieces and add it to the egg mixture.
4. Add salt and pepper to taste.
5. Pour the mixture into your mug.
6. Microwave for 1 1/2 to 2 minutes. Check the omelette after each 15-second interval until cooked to your preference.
7. Enjoy your omelette immediately!

Eggless Chocolate Mug Cake

Servings 1 | Time| 05 minutes

Nutritional Content

Cal 476 | Fat 23.1 g | Protein 6.7g | Carbs 68 g| Fiber | 4.1 g

Ingredients

- ❖ 30 g (¼ cup) almond flour
- ❖ 45 g (3 tablespoons) coconut Sugar
- ❖ 15 g (2 tablespoons) Cocoa Powder
- ❖ 1 g (¼ teaspoon) Baking Soda

- ❖ Salt a pinch of
- ❖ 45 ml (3 tablespoons) coconut Milk
- ❖ 20 ml (1 ½ tablespoons) Vegetable Oil

Directions

1. In a microwave-safe mug, combine flour, coconut sugar, cocoa powder, baking soda, and salt.
2. Add milk and vegetable oil, and stir until there are no more clumps. Mix in milk chocolate.
3. Microwave for 60 to 90 seconds. Cooking time will vary depending on the wattage of your microwave.
4. Once cooked, sprinkle with icing sugar and enjoy immediately.

Veggie Mug Omelette

Servings 1 | Time| 05 minutes

Nutritional Content

Cal 295 | Fat 15.9 g | Protein 19.7 g | Carbs 21 g| Fiber | 3.6 g

Ingredients

- ❖ 2 large eggs
- ❖ 30 mL (2 Tbsp.) milk
- ❖ 30 g (2 Tbsp.) shredded cheddar cheese
- ❖ 20 g (2 Tbsp.) finely diced pepper
- ❖ 20 g (2 Tbsp) finely diced pepper
- ❖ 10 g (¼ cup) roughly chopped fresh spinach
- ❖ Salt and pepper, to taste

Directions

1. Lightly grease a large coffee mug.
2. Combine milk and eggs in the mug and stir. Then, mix in the cheese, peppers, and spinach.
3. Microwave the egg on high for 1-2 minutes, stirring at 30-second intervals.
4. Serve hot and add salt and pepper to taste.

Coffee Cup Quiche

Servings 1 | Time|10 minutes

Nutritional Content

Cal 42 | Fat 0.6 g | Protein 0.3 g | Carbs 9.1 g| Fiber | 0.1 g

Ingredients

- ❖ 1 egg
- ❖ 20 g (1 1/2 tablespoons) milk
- ❖ Salt
- ❖ Ground black pepper
- ❖ 1/4 of a bagel

- ❖ 10 g (2 teaspoons) cream cheese
- ❖ 1/2 slice prosciutto or ham
- ❖ Fresh thyme leaves or fresh chopped chives
- ❖ Dijon mustard

Directions

1. To prepare, mix egg and milk in a coffee cup. Add salt and pepper to taste.
2. Break bread into small pieces and add to the mixture.
3. Combine cream cheese and diced prosciutto.
4. Add thyme.
5. Microwave for 1 minute and 10 seconds on high.
6. Garnish with fresh chives or thyme and mustard.

Egg Mug Muffin

Servings 1 | Time|10 minutes

Nutritional Content

Cal 313 | Fat 15.6 g | Protein 10.3 g | Carbs 32.7 g| Fiber | 1.1 g

Ingredients

- ❖ 40 g (5 tablespoons) plain flour
- ❖ 1 g (¼ teaspoon) baking powder
- ❖ ½ g (⅛ teaspoon) baking soda
- ❖ ½ g (⅛ teaspoon salt
- ❖ 30 ml (2 tablespoons) milk
- ❖ 10 ml (2 teaspoons) vegetable oil or melted butter
- ❖ 30 g (2 tablespoons) egg
- ❖ 15 g (1 tablespoon) grated cheddar cheese
- ❖ 15 g (1 tablespoon) spring onion chopped
- ❖ 1 small egg

Directions

1. Combine flour, baking soda, baking powder, and salt in a microwave-safe mug using a fork.
2. Add milk, oil, egg, cheese, and scallions and stir until everything is mixed.
3. Create a well in the centre of the batter with a spoon and add the egg.
4. Spoon the remaining batter from the edges over the egg. It may be a little challenging, but you can do it.
5. Microwave for 50-110 seconds until the top is firm to the touch. Cooking time may vary depending on your microwave's wattage. Keep a close eye on your mug to prevent spills or overcooking.

Meatloaf in a Mug

Servings 36 | Time| 30 minutes

Nutritional Content

Cal 394 | Fat 8.5 g | Protein 39.9 g | Carbs 37.6 g| Fiber | 3.7 g

Ingredients

- ❖ 30 ml (2 tablespoons) water
- ❖ 15 g (1 tablespoon) tomato paste
- ❖ 10 g (2 tablespoons) quinoa
- ❖ 4 g (1 teaspoon) soup mix
- ❖ 115 g (1/4 pound) ground chicken

Directions

1. In a mixing bowl, combine quinoa, tomato paste, water, and soup mix.
2. Stir in crumbled meat and transfer the mixture to a microwave-safe cup or custard mug.
3. Microwave the chicken, covered, on high for about three minutes after draining.
4. Let it sit for three minutes and top the dish with more ketchup, if desired.

Cheesy homemade grits

Servings 36 | Time| 30 minutes

Nutritional Content

Cal 242 | Fat 21.2 g | Protein7.7 g | Carbs 6.3 g| Fiber | 1 g

Ingredients

- ❖ 240 ml (1 cup) of water
- ❖ 40 g (1/4 cup) grits
- ❖ Kosher salt
- ❖ 5 g (1 tsp) Butter
- ❖ 15 g (1 tbsp.) Shredded cheddar cheese

Directions

1. Mix water, grits, and salt in a microwave-safe mug.
2. Microwave on high for five minutes, then stir.
3. If needed, microwave for an additional 1-minute interval until desired consistency is reached.
4. Add butter and cheese after removing from microwave.
5. Enjoy your delicious grits.

Sweet potato hash

Servings 1 | Time| 10 minutes

Nutritional Content

Cal 116 | Fat 4.8 g | Protein 4.9 g | Carbs 13.7 g| Fiber | 2.3 g

Ingredients

- ❖ 60 g (1 small) sweet potato (around 1 cup), peeled and cubed
- ❖ Water, enough to cover the potatoes
- ❖ 2 peppers, chopped

- ❖ 10 g (1 tablespoon) red onion, chopped
- ❖ 30 g (2 tablespoons) grated cheese
- ❖ A pinch of salt and pepper
- ❖ 10 g (2 teaspoon) rosemary, fresh or dried

Directions

1. Fill a microwave-safe cup with sweet potato cubes and water up to the top.
2. Microwave on high for 3-4 minutes. Once done, remove the cup and drain the water.
3. Add and microwave the remaining ingredients on high for 40 seconds.
4. Enjoy!

Chicken noodle soup

Servings 1 | Time| 15 minutes

Nutritional Content

Cal 275 | Fat 7.6 g | Protein 28 g | Carbs 22.1 g| Fiber | 3.3 g

Ingredients

- ❖ 240 ml (1 cup) chicken broth
- ❖ 70 g (½ cup) shredded rotisserie or roasted chicken (skin removed)
- ❖ 30 g (¼ cup) very thinly sliced carrots
- ❖ 40 g (¼ cup) cooked small egg noodles
- ❖ 15 g (1 tablespoon) thinly sliced trimmed spring onion
- ❖ 4 g (1 teaspoon) fresh lemon juice
- ❖ ½ g (⅛ teaspoon) kosher salt
- ❖ 2 grinds of black pepper
- ❖ 5 g (1 tablespoon) finely chopped fresh dill or parsley

Directions

1. In a large microwave-safe mug, mix the broth, chicken, noodles, scallions, juice, salt, and pepper.
2. Microwave on high for 7 minutes.
3. Remove from the microwave, add parsley or dill as a garnish, and savor.

Printed in Great Britain
by Amazon

40720142R00077